# TURN YOUR CUSTOMERS

# INTO YOUR SALES FORCE

### The Art of Winning Repeat and Referral Customers

# ROSS R. RECK

PRENTICE
HALL
PRESS

NEW YORK   LONDON   TORONTO   SYDNEY   TOKYO   SINGAPORE

**Prentice Hall Press**
15 Columbus Circle
New York, NY 10023

Copyright © 1991 by Ross R. Reck

PRENTICE HALL PRESS and colophons are registered trademarks
of Simon & Schuster, Inc.

**Library of Congress Cataloging-in-Publication Data**

Reck, Ross Richard, 1945–
Turn your customers into your sales force / Ross R. Reck.
p.     cm.
Includes index.
ISBN 0-13-435165-7
1. Sales management.   2. Customer satisfaction.   I. Title.
HF5438.4.R42   1991
658.8'12—dc20               90-43928
                                              CIP

Designed by Irving Perkins Associates

Manufactured in the United States of America

10   9   8   7   6   5   4   3   2

First Edition

*To Marcia, Philip, Katie, and Nancy,*
*the best family anyone could ever have.*

# ACKNOWLEDGMENTS

JOYCE and ANGELO KINICKI, MARY NORFLEET, and DICK and ROBIN BELTRAMINI, for their great support and encouragement.

BRIAN LONG, my coauthor on *The Win-Win Negotiator*, for his contributions in developing the PRAM Model.

JIM WOODSON for helping me see the world through a clearer set of eyes.

KEN BLANCHARD, coauthor of *The One Minute Manager*, for his inspiration and for serving as a role model.

TONY RANDALL, actor, who provided me with the insight into the true meaning of negotiation.

JANE DYSTEL, my literary agent, and PAUL ARON, my editor, for their excellent efforts in helping to pull this project together.

# CONTENTS

# INTRODUCTION

Like it or not, every one of us is a salesperson. It's a fact of life. We're all selling something whether it be our friendship, an idea, a point of view, a product, or a professional service. The people to whom we try to sell these things are our customers. This means that our success is directly related to our ability to get our customers to buy whatever we are selling.

The success of attorneys, consultants, and other professionals is dependent on their ability to develop and maintain a client base. The success of physicians, dentists, and psychologists depends on their ability to attract and maintain a cadre of regular patients. Directors and CEOs depend on their ability to build and maintain a base of influence within their respective organizations. And the success of professional salespeople and account representatives is directly related to their ability to attract and maintain a base of committed buyers.

Although every one of us sells something every day, it is not easy to do well. Standard methods of selling often leave us unhappy, burned out, or rejected—and very often all three.

Many salespeople today find themselves frustrated. Most of what they learn from books and seminars about selling does not match what their hearts tell them is right. What's even worse is that these methods don't work very well. By and large, salespeople are taught that the name of the game in selling is to get the order and they are to do whatever it takes to achieve this end. If this means using techniques that smack of manipulation, con, deception, or even intimidation, then so be it—but get the order!

The problem with this traditional "Win-Lose" method of selling is that it views each sale as an isolated event. This means that every time a salesperson wants another dollar, he or she has to close another sale. And since most people strongly resent being manipulated or deceived, salespeople who apply these Win-Lose methods experience very low success rates. They have to make an inordinate number of sales calls in order to make up for all the rejections they encounter. Clearly, pursuing such a course of action as a salesperson is a sure ticket to a high level of stress and eventual burnout.

But take heart, there is an alternative! For now, let's call it the "Win-Win" method of selling. Salespeople who apply this method take a longer-term view of the selling process. They don't just want their customers to buy on a one-time basis. Rather, they make their customers feel so good about their buying experiences that these customers continue to buy, and they feel compelled to tell others. In other words, Win-Win salespeople are not after the order, they're after the *business.* As a result, they don't have to pound the pavement or experience the rejection that Win-Lose salespeople do; they have their satisfied customers who, in turn, sell for them. They are actually managing their customers as their own personal sales force!

Turning your customers into your sales force means you work smarter, not harder. Joe Girard got into the *Guinness Book of World Records* as the "World's Number-One New Car Salesman" by selling 1,425 new cars in one year. He is quick to point out that 65 percent of his sales was repeat business. Given the high level of regard his customers had for him, the other 35 percent of his sales was probably the result of referrals from his satisfied customers. So in reality Joe Girard actually sold very few cars that year. He was a master of working smarter, not harder.

This book will show you how to work smarter instead

of harder as a salesperson, regardless of who your customers are. The Win-Win method of selling described in this book works equally well in all sales situations, whether you're a professional salesperson, attorney, dentist, or CEO. Even though every sales transaction is different, the basic elements involved do not change. The payoff for using this method of selling is simple: You'll be more successful with less effort, but most important, you'll feel good about yourself.

# TURN YOUR CUSTOMERS INTO YOUR SALES FORCE

# CHAPTER ONE

# Positioning Yourself for Success

WHEN I SPEAK of highly successful people, I'm not referring to people who inherited their wealth or people whose lottery ticket happened to hit. Rather, I'm talking about people like you and me who are responsible for their own success—however each of us chooses to define success. In doing the research for this book, whenever I talked to others about highly successful people, the comment I heard most often was something like, "Wow! That person really has what it takes."

In almost all cases, the characteristics that seemed to separate these highly successful people from the masses was a magical quality called "it." Everyone was quick to point out that highly successful people possessed this quality, but no one could explain to me what "it" was.

As I pressed for specifics, I found the answers fell into three categories. The first category was that these highly successful people have an *amazing ability to draw other people to them*—a magnetic personality, if you will. In other words, if these people were selling something, customers seemed to jump out of the woodwork just for a chance to buy from them.

Although this ability may sound wonderful at first, being able to draw other people toward you sounds more like an ability you would inherit than an ability that you could learn. So I said to myself, there has to be a more concrete answer to this question, something that interested people can more easily sink their teeth into.

The next category of answer was that these people have an *unbelievable ability to get other people to go the extra mile on their behalf.* This answer interested me, because as any successful person eventually learns, success in this life is not tied so much to what you can do for yourself as to what you can get others to do on your behalf. If you try to do everything by yourself, you very quickly find yourself constrained by the limitations of what one person can physically accomplish. On the other hand, if you can enlist the active support of others, your potential becomes virtually unlimited. I liked what I was hearing in this answer, but I was still convinced that a better answer was possible, so I continued my search.

The next category of answer was the one that grabbed me. It said that these highly successful people have a *wonderful ability to get other people to stand in line just for the privilege of doing them a favor!* As simplistic as this might sound, this was the common thread that tied all highly successful people together. They all had a whole army of people chafing at the bit for the opportunity to do something nice for them. This is what the rest of this book is all about. It will give you the specifics of how you can get your customers (those people on whom you are dependent for your success) to stand in line just waiting for the chance to do you a favor. The process highly successful people use to get people to enthusiastically go the extra mile on their behalf is called Win-Win Negotiation.

# CHAPTER TWO

# Win-Win Negotiating

WHENEVER I MENTION that the ability to negotiate is critical to success as a salesperson, I am almost always met with raised eyebrows. And the reason for this is that negotiation is probably the most misunderstood concept in North America. Most people tend to view negotiation as some sort of semi-ethical process that is designed to con, manipulate, or intimidate another person into saying yes when they really want to say no.

In order to clear up this misunderstanding, when I'm conducting a seminar or giving a speech, I usually put the attendees through a short exercise. I describe some situations to these people and I ask them to tell me which of the situations involves negotiation. When I ask them if they think the reaching of a labor agreement between the United Auto Workers and Ford Motor Company would involve negotiation, all of the hands in the room go up. Similarly, when I ask if the reaching of a nuclear arms reduction agreement between the United States and the Soviet Union would involve negotiation, everyone raises their hand. When I ask them if getting their children to make their bed or clean their room involves negotiation, I get a few laughs, but again, all raise their hands.

At this point, I tell the attendees that what they have just indicated, by raising their hands, is that nearly all human interaction involves some element of negotiation. Furthermore, their success in any of these situations is directly related to their ability to negotiate with different people. It is now obvious that a person's ability to negotiate plays a key role in determining his or her level of success. The problem, however, is that if I were to poll any 100 people and ask them their personal definitions of negotiation, chances are I would get 100 different definitions. This definition issue is precisely the stumbling block that prevents people from achieving higher levels of success. Indeed, it's very difficult to do something well if you're not quite sure what it is you are supposed to do.

In order to clear up this definition problem I fell back on my ten years' experience as a professor. One of the things I learned early in that career is that whenever confusion exists concerning what something is or should be, it's very helpful to go back and take a look at the origins of the word itself. In doing this, very often what you find is that the original meaning of the word and what has subsequently evolved are often two entirely different things. It turned out that this was also true for the word *negotiation.*

If you take a look at any standard dictionary, you'll find that the root word of negotiation is the Latin word *otio.* Otio means that a human being is at a state of leisure. When you are on a vacation or otherwise relaxed and enjoying yourself, you are at otio. As far as the Latin language is concerned, human beings can only be at one of two states. They are either at otio, meaning they are relaxing and enjoying themselves, or they are at the opposite state from otio: conducting business. The way you would write the opposite of otio in Latin is simply *neg otio.*

So, literally translated from Latin, negotiation means

"not leisure," or "to conduct business." It is interesting to note that "to conduct business" is the precise definition of negotiation that you will find in any dictionary, but very few people have ever bothered to look it up—even people teaching workshops and seminars on negotiation.

The reason for taking you through the above analysis is to point out two very important aspects of negotiation. First, negotiation does not mean a process whereby you try to manipulate, con, or intimidate someone into saying yes when they really want to say no, although this is one of the more common misconceptions about the negotiation process.

Second, negotiation is a *people* process. People are the only entities capable of promising things to each other and they are the only entities capable of following through on those promises. Companies do not negotiate with companies. For example, a company like IBM does not negotiate a sales transaction with a company like Exxon. For such a transaction to occur, someone or a group of people representing IBM would negotiate with someone or a group of people representing Exxon. The quality of the agreements themselves, as well as the quality of the follow-through on those agreements, would be directly related to the quality of the personal relationships between the people involved. People do things for people, they don't do things for companies or agencies. Furthermore, people are very willing to go the extra mile for people they like and trust, but they rarely, if ever, stick their necks out for people they don't like or trust. As one very successful businessman said when he was addressing a roomful of branch managers from Bank of America, "You people have to remember that people don't bank with banks, they bank with people." He went on to say, "To the average consumer, banks all look the same. What makes one bank stand out from the others is the quality of the personal treatment you get from the people with whom you come into contact."

Therefore, the definition of negotiation that I will use for the rest of this book is *a basic process of getting what you want from other people.* If you get your children to make their beds or clean their rooms, that's getting what you want from other people. Similarly, if you want other people to stand in line just for the privilege of doing you a favor, that's getting what you want from other people. Most important, if you want your customers to remain loyal, give you lots of repeat business, and refer their friends to you, that's also getting what you want from other people. As such, negotiation is *the* fundamental activity involved in the sales process. Thus, in order to achieve a high level of success as a salesperson, you must become an effective negotiator.

Now that we understand what negotiation is, let's take a look at the two basic philosophies that people utilize to get what they want from other people. The first of these philosophies is the Win-Win Philosophy and the other is the Win-Lose Philosophy.

## THE WIN-WIN PHILOSOPHY

The idea behind the Win-Win Philosophy is that I get what I want by helping others get what they want and vice versa. In a true Win-Win sales transaction, both parties come away feeling very good about the deal they have just concluded. Both are likely to follow through on their respective promises, to look forward to doing business together again in the future, and to refer others.

For example, a senior vice-president of a bank for whom I was doing some consulting came to me one day crying the blues. His concern was that some of the competing banks had decided aggressively to go after some of the large depositors who did business with his branch banks located in several wealthy retirement communities. The way in which these competing banks were trying to lure these wealthy customers away was by offering them significantly higher interest rates if they would switch banks. The senior vice-president went on to say he felt that the only way he could hang onto these very important customers was to match or beat the higher rates being offered by his competitors. He was reluctant to do this, however, because it would be expensive and it would probably trigger a price war that would eventually result in none of the competitors making any money.

I suggested that if he didn't want to lose these valuable customers, he'd have to give them a reason to stay. I went on to tell him that matching the competition on interest was one way to do this, but it was probably not getting at the real reason these people were leaving. I pointed out that wealthy people like to be treated in a special manner that singles them out. And I suggested that probably all of these people already had more than enough money to last them for the rest of their lives, so a few dollars more was not likely to be a long-term motivator of their behavior.

I suggested he give these wealthier depositors some very special attention and basically ignore the interest rate increases being offered by the competition. We came up with a program to organize gala events for these people on a quarterly basis—elegant afternoon tea parties, for example. These parties were announced to the targeted customers using engraved invitations. The tea and hors d'oeuvres were served with fine china and silver. In addition, the president of the bank or one of the officers was on hand at each of these events to mingle with the guests.

These tea parties have been a smashing success. Instead of losing any of these wealthy customers, the bank actually began to attract new customers as the result of referrals from people who had attended some of the parties. This was truly Win-Win in action: The customers got what they wanted—special treatment that appealed to their egos—and the senior vice-president got what he wanted, in that he was able to hang onto these customers without having to match the interest rates being offered by the competition. The cost of the parties was insignificant compared to the cost of meeting the competition's higher rates.

## THE WIN-LOSE PHILOSOPHY

The Win-Lose Philosophy of getting what you want from other people is simply, "I get what I want from you at your expense." In other words, I win and you lose and *you know it*. The problem with applying this philosophy is that it does not motivate other people to stand in line just for the privilege of doing you a favor. Rather, it motivates people to go out of their way to get even. The problem is compounded by the fact that when people are motivated to get even, they don't do it all by themselves. They unite their friends against you. So, instead of alienating one person with your Win-Lose behavior, you have a whole army of people looking for a chance to do you in. Dr. Kevin Leman from Tucson says that grandparents and grandchildren get along so well for a similar reason—they have a common enemy!

Two years ago on Memorial Day weekend, my family and I went to a local dealership to look at new cars. This started out as one of the most pleasant buying experiences that has ever happened to me. The salesperson did something for me that no other car salesperson had ever done before. Instead of trying to sell me a car, he let me buy one! For several hours, we got into and out of a fair number of cars and went on several test drives. All the while, this salesperson patiently showed us around and courteously answered our questions until we finally came across a car that everyone liked.

At this point, the whole family said, "We'll take it!" The salesperson was appreciative and informed me that his role in the sales transaction ended at this point and that now he would turn me over to the finance person who would get our loan approved. Since I had such a positive experience with the salesperson, I was sure that my experience with the finance person would be equally positive. Was I in for a shock!

The finance person we dealt with would have been at home on any sleazy used car lot. He talked a mile a minute while he processed the information for the standard contract form. Once the form was completed, he passed it through a slot in the wall to another person who would match up a financial institution with our loan application. He then told us to have a seat until the loan was approved, which would probably take half an hour.

Forty-five minutes later, he called us back into his office and enthusiastically informed us that our loan was approved at an interest rate of 15.11 percent. I asked him if that interest rate wasn't a little on the high side. His response was, "Oh no, that's what banks are getting these days for new car loans."

I looked him in the eye and asked him, "You wouldn't lie to me, would you?"

The finance person responded, "No way!"

I then explained to him that I was a consultant to one of the larger banks in town and that I had a meeting scheduled on the next business day with one of its vice-presidents. I asked the finance person to hold our loan application until I had a chance to find out for myself if the 15.11 percent he was trying to charge me was legitimate. He must have thought I was bluffing because he didn't try very hard to talk me out of what I had proposed.

I met with the bank vice-president and found out that 11.9 percent financing was available for new car loans. With this information, I went back to the car dealer to have a discussion with the finance person. As I walked into his office, I waved the bank vice-president's business card and informed him that 11.9 percent financing was available. At this point, he reluctantly inserted a new contract form into his computerized typewriter and said, "Well, if you want 11.9, you've got 11.9!"

Doing a little leg work had kept me from being taken advantage of, but the very idea that this dealership had tried to take advantage of me in the first place left a bad taste in my mouth. During the next two years, nine of my friends bought cars similar to mine. Each of them asked me, before they went looking, where I bought my car and what kind of experience I had. I emphatically told each of these friends to avoid like the plague the dealer where I had bought my car. Had this dealership treated me with fairness and dignity instead of trying to con me, it could have chalked up nine additional sales. The profit on these nine additional sales would have been far more than the dealership would have made had it succeeded in conning me. What's more, the dealership wouldn't have had to sell these nine additional cars. If my experience had been positive, I would have sold these nine cars for the dealership!

It should be obvious at this point that if you want to be really successful as a salesperson, you *must* adopt the Win-Win Philosophy.

# CHAPTER THREE

# PRAM: Plans, Relationships, Agreements, and Maintenance

THIS CHAPTER INTRODUCES a model of the Win-Win Negotiation process. This is the same model featured in the book *The Win-Win Negotiator*, which I coauthored with Brian G. Long. After an explanation of the model, I will show how it applies directly to the selling process.

As you look at the model on the next page, the first thing you should notice is that it is circular. This is because negotiation is a continuous process. You have to remember that you are dealing with people and that you cannot turn human feelings and emotions on and off like a light switch. Once you begin negotiating with another human being, you continue to do so until you terminate the relationship.

The second thing you should notice about the model is that there are four parts. PRAM is an acronym for these four steps of negotiating: Plans, Relationships, Agreements, and Maintenance. Let's take a look now at each of these four steps.

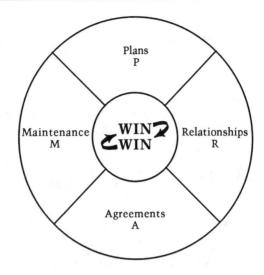

THE PRAM MODEL:
THE WIN-WIN NEGOTIATION PROCESS

## PLANS

The first step in the Win-Win Negotiation process is the development of a Win-Win Plan. The essence of a Win-Win Plan answers the question: "What can I do for the person I'm about to deal with that will motivate that person to give me what I want in return?" I used to think that negotiation was a give-and-take process, but in reality there is no such thing as taking: You can only motivate other people to give. Looking at negotiation as a give-and-take process is like viewing a marriage as a 50:50 proposition. The problem with viewing a marriage in this manner is that you spend the majority of time arguing over where your 50 stops and your spouse's 50 starts. On the other hand, if you view a marriage as a 100:100 proposition, where both parties concentrate on the giving, the taking then takes care of itself.

Cynics are quick to dismiss the notion of Win-Win

planning saying that it's not "real world," or that it may work well when times are good and there's lots of money to spread around, but that it doesn't hold water when times are tough and money is scarce. Well, let me assure you that Win-Win is "real world" and when times are tough, approaching problems from a Win-Win perspective is probably the one thing that will save your neck!

For example, several years ago I became involved with a copper mining company that owned a mine which had been shut down due to depressed copper prices. As a result, people were moving away from this small company town in droves and there was speculation that the town would have to close the high school and bus the students to a community located fifty miles away. Needless to say, morale in this community was at an all-time low.

As I talked to the mine's general manager, he explained to me that as gloomy as the situation looked, there was still a glimmer of hope. He believed that if they could figure out a way to reduce the cost of producing a pound of copper by eight cents, then mining the copper would be profitable and they could reopen the mine. His plan was to save five of the needed eight cents by putting in newer and more efficient processing equipment. My job was to show the purchasing department how to negotiate the remaining three cents away from their suppliers—vendors who supplied the mines with materials and services.

The general manager then introduced me to the people in the mine's purchasing department. The first question I asked the head of the purchasing department was how he and his department planned to save the additional three cents per pound. He reluctantly told me that they had already resorted twice to the only solution they knew: bring in their suppliers and beat them down. This meant the suppliers would do all the giving and the mine would do all the taking, clearly a Win-Lose situation.

I asked the head of the department if he and his people were looking forward to this experience. The head of the department answered in frustration, "Are you kidding?

We've already beaten them down twice. Some of these people are losing money the way it is. And we're supposed to ask them for further price reductions? They're going to be hostile!"

After hearing the rest of the department vent similar frustrations, I suggested a fresh approach—Win-Win. I drew the PRAM Model on the chalkboard and spent the next two hours talking about each of the four steps. At the end of the two hours, from the comments I was hearing, I was convinced these people understood Win-Win. I then walked over to a flip chart, grabbed a magic marker and said, "Now I want you to give me your Win-Win ideas; things that you can do for your suppliers who are already losing money and who are in some cases hostile, that will motivate them to enthusiastically volunteer even further price reductions."

Much to my disappointment, the room fell deadly silent. So silent, in fact, that I began to think it was time for me to consider a career change. Finally, the warehouse foreman raised his hand to suggest an idea. He knew for a fact that the mining company paid fifteen cents a gallon less for its diesel fuel than the trucking company that hauled the mine's concentrated ore to the smelter some three hundred miles away. He suggested that the mining company purchase the fuel for the trucking company if the trucking company would agree to pass some of the savings back in the form of lower prices. I told this man that he had a great idea and suggested that his company not try to hang onto all the fifteen cents. If he wanted to show good faith and get the trucking company to actively work toward getting the mine back open, he should split the fifteen cents with the trucking company. In this manner, the trucking company could lower its price for its services and, at the same time, increase its profits—truly a Win-Win proposition.

All of a sudden everyone in the room had their hands up. Win-Win ideas, which initially seemed so foreign to these people, were coming at me so quickly that I couldn't write fast enough on the flip chart to keep up. As a result of that session, the purchasing department not only saved the three cents per pound they were looking for, they saved nearly four cents, and without any hostile confrontations with their suppliers. As the head of the department put it, "For the first time, bringing our suppliers in under very adverse circumstances to talk about a very touchy subject was fun." The mine opened up two months later—a very happy ending.

As you can see, if you take Win-Win seriously, you can turn even the most dire of circumstances into a glowing success story.

## RELATIONSHIPS

Once you've established your Win-Win Plan, you come to a step in the Win-Win Negotiation process that is often ignored: the development of Win-Win personal relationships. Developing these relationships is critical because people are very willing to go that extra mile for someone they like and trust. On the other hand, people will rarely stick their neck out for someone they don't like or don't trust. What you're trying to develop is the mutual assurance that if you do a favor for someone today, you can rest assured that when you ask that same person for a favor sometime in the future, the answer is going to be yes.

The way you develop these relationships is by spending some time visiting the people you deal with prior to asking them for anything. This allows you to get to know them and them to get to know you. You can use opportunities like lunch, informal visits, golf, and so on to allow this to happen. Use this time to communicate that you are an honest and trustworthy individual. This step is critical, because without trust you'll never get genuine commitment from the people you're dealing with.

Eighty to 90 percent of the people who go into the

business of selling insurance leave the field within a year. Let's take a look at a typical beginning insurance salesperson: Jill, a college graduate who has just completed an insurance company's three-week training program at corporate headquarters.

After Jill has completed her training program, the first person to whom she tries to sell a policy is her father—*someone with whom she has an already-established relationship.* Now he probably needs another insurance policy like he needs a hole in his head, but he wants Jill to get off to a good start. After the transaction has been completed and Jill has a check from her father, he says, "I'll bet your brother could use some insurance." Of course her brother, in the interest of maintaining peace in the family, will eventually say yes. And finally, everybody like Jill has a few friends who would rather write her a check for a few hundred dollars than risk losing her as a friend.

Eventually, however, Jill runs out of friends and relatives—people with whom she has already-existing relationships. When this happens, she tries the same techniques on total strangers that worked on her father and she experiences doors slamming in her face. Regardless of how strong a person's self-image is, there are a finite number of door slams that a person can endure. When this occurs, Jill decides that maybe she isn't cut out to sell insurance and changes careers.

It's interesting to contrast the Jills of this world with those people who go into the business of selling insurance, make a career out of it, get rich at it, and eventually turn the business over to their children. The only thing these people do differently is to *invest*, up front, in relationships and then spend the time and effort to maintain these relationships. After a certain amount of time, they no longer have to sell insurance. The reason: *Their satisfied customers are selling it for them!*

In his book, *Thriving on Chaos*, Tom Peters talks about how a Lutheran minister in a small town in Pennsylvania used relationship development to solidify his parish and increase church attendance. When this minister first took over his parish, he shocked the local people by practicing Ministry by Wandering Around, by being the first minister in twenty years to visit the local coffee shop and have coffee with the farmers. As the minister put it, "By stopping at the coffee shop, I build relationships." This minister also visits each of his parishioners' homes once a year because he has found that people speak more freely on their home turf. As a result of these activities, attendance at Sunday services quickly shot up by 25 percent.

## AGREEMENTS

Once the relationship is in place, the next step in the process is forming a Win-Win Agreement. In it I offer to give you what you want in exchange for your giving me what I want. What's important to note here is that if the first two steps of the Win-Win process have been executed correctly; i.e., the planning has been done from a Win-Win perspective and a genuinely trusting relationship has been developed, then reaching an agreement is merely a matter of working out the details. Discussions are conducted in an open atmosphere and take on a character of, "I can do this if you can do that."

An article in the April 1988 issue of *Nation's Business* talked about how Sam Walton, then chairman of Wal-Mart stores, and his staff went about forming Win-Win Agreements with some of their suppliers. According to the article, in late 1984 the governor of Arkansas called Wal-Mart's president and asked for help in saving Farris Fashions, a struggling shirt manufacturing company in eastern Arkansas. This company had made Van Heusen shirts for years, but Van Heusen had recently pulled its contract and gone overseas with it. It was the governor's view that Farris Fashions had potential; it also had ninety employees looking for something to do.

Walton, his president, and several other executives mulled the situation over and decided to try to help this company. At the time, Wal-Mart was buying the printed flannel shirts it sold in its stores from manufacturers in the Far East. This appeared to be the type of product that Farris Fashions was capable of making. So a phone call was made to the president of Farris Fashions and a meeting was set up. The Wal-Mart executives stated that they would be happy to buy some of their printed flannel shirts from Farris, but Farris would have to be competitive in quality and price with the Far East.

After several such meetings, the Farris president said that his company could be competitive with the Far East, but it would require that he make a major investment in new equipment to make his operation more efficient. He would also need to get his suppliers to lower their prices on the materials he purchased, such as flannel, buttons, and lining. The Farris president went on to say that he could do all this if he could get a large-scale purchase commitment from Wal-Mart, if Wal-Mart would agree to pay its invoices immediately upon receipt of the goods, and if Wal-Mart could use its large-scale purchasing power to help secure a good price on the flannel used in the shirts.

After some discussion, the Wal-Mart executives decided that if Farris could be competitive with the Far East in quality and price, Wal-Mart would consider committing to buy 240,000 printed flannel shirts for the first order, see that Farris received payment within ten days of the receipt of the merchandise (instead of the standard thirty to ninety days), and investigate what they could do about the price of flannel.

With Wal-Mart's commitment, the Farris president was able to go to his suppliers for buttons, linings, labels, and so forth to see if they could lower their prices, given this large volume. He didn't approach his suppliers with an attitude of trying to chisel or demand a lower price from them. Rather, he approached them with an attitude of "What can you suppliers do to help me win this contract from Wal-Mart in such a way that each supplier would still make a fair return for his effort." Furthermore, he told them that if their cooperative effort was successful and Farris did win the contract, those suppliers who helped would be guaranteed the business. This, in turn, motivated Farris's suppliers to look for creative ways of lowering their prices without endangering their product quality or profit margin. For example, one supplier said he had just run into a bargain and would be happy to pass some of these savings on to Farris in order to help them win the contract.

Armed with these lower material prices, it was time for another meeting with Wal-Mart. At the meeting it was learned that Wal-Mart had been able to secure a very good price for flannel from a source in Asia and that Wal-Mart itself would buy the flannel for Farris. With this final piece of information, Farris was able to put together a price for these shirts that was more than competitive with the Far East. The result: Farris was awarded the contract.

Four years later, Farris had supplied 1.5 million garments (mostly men's and boy's shirts) to Wal-Mart. Farris had installed more than a million dollars' worth of new equipment and had grown from 90 to 325 employees.

On the other hand, if the planning has been one-sided and the relationship is nonexistent or antagonistic, then attempting to reach an agreement becomes a free-for-all.

A good example of such a free-for-all occurred in the fall of 1987 when the National Football League Player's Association was trying to negotiate an acceptable labor agreement with the owners of the NFL teams. This was a classic case of how *not* to negotiate. First of all, both parties to the negotiation planned from a one-sided perspective. Each knew what it wanted from the negotiation, but neither was the least bit concerned with what the other party wanted. Second, the players resented the owners because the owners had lied to them on numerous occasions. On the other side, the owners resented the players for trying to exert more and more control over the game itself as well as the revenue stream associated with professional football.

The owners felt that control over these aspects of the game rightfully belonged to them. These mutual feelings of resentment were dramatically intensified by the media because of their eagerness to hype every rumor and embellish every off-the-cuff comment.

To make matters worse, several weeks into the regular season the players decided to go on strike, calculating that the lost revenue would force the owners to be more accommodating to the wants and needs of the players. The owners countered by hiring non-union players and playing the games anyway, sending a clear message to the union players that the game of professional football could get along without them.

To say that the relationship between these two parties was antagonistic would have been an understatement. It's almost absurd to think that these two parties would even try to hammer out an acceptable agreement under such circumstances, but try they did—and they failed miserably. The three weeks or so of the strike cost the players and owners collectively $205 million dollars and not one single thing was accomplished!

Although this situation was an extreme case, it does point out some of the problems you can encounter when you try to reach agreements without having done your planning from a Win-Win perspective, and without having established a solid relationship of trust.

## MAINTENANCE

Once an agreement has been formed and both parties part company with a solid commitment to follow through, there is still much that needs to be done. As any successful salesperson will tell you, the sale really begins after the sale. The reason is that you want customers to come back, and you also want them to bring their friends. Three things need to be maintained: the agreement, the relationship, and the plan.

**Maintaining the Agreement (Commitment)**

Maintaining an agreement involves two activities. First, and most immediately, make sure you hold up your end of the agreement. Nothing will diminish commitment faster than your not holding up your end of the agreement. If you don't hold up your end, there is no incentive for the other party to hold up its end of the agreement, and the whole agreement is in danger of falling apart.

It is critical, especially for people with whom the relationship is new, that you seize the first opportunity, after you've reached an agreement, to communicate strongly that you intend to follow through with a high level of enthusiasm. This communication need only take the form of summarizing what was discussed during the meeting on a piece of paper and mailing it to the other party that same day, or calling the other party on the following day to let him or her know you've already begun to follow through on what you promised. This will communicate to the other party that you are a person of your word and that his or her needs, which are covered in the agreement, are going to be met. The other party now has every incentive to hold up his or her end of the agreement.

Several years ago I was flying on American Airlines from Albany, New York, through Chicago's O'Hare Airport to Phoenix. The flight out of Albany was two hours late because of a mechanical problem, which meant I would miss my connection on the last flight of the evening to Phoenix and have to spend the night in Chicago. As the plane taxied up to the gate, I asked one of the flight attendants what kind of treatment I could expect from American Airlines: would they treat me with a sense of appreciation as I had just gone the extra mile for American Airlines, or would they give me a meal ticket for the employees' cafeteria and tell me to wait at the airport until the next flight left in the morning? The flight attendant's response was, "I don't know. That's not my end of the business. But good luck." Needless to say, I had visions of a long and uncomfortable night in Chicago.

I got to the American Airlines ticket counter at about 10:30 P.M. expecting the very worst. A very sympathetic and pleasant ticket agent greeted me and when I told him my name, he immediately gave me my boarding pass for the morning flight, handed me a voucher for the Westin O'Hare, pointed to where the limousine would pick me up in two to three minutes, and said, "I am very sorry for any inconvenience this has caused you."

Talk about a pleasant surprise! I was absolutely shocked. The whole transaction took forty-five seconds and the treatment was strictly first class, as the room at the Westin was incredibly expensive. I learned that American Airlines enjoyed a substantial discount rate for a block of rooms at the Westin O'Hare that was set aside for passengers who missed their flights. Because it was nearly Christmas and Chicago was jammed with people, all the hotels in town were full, with people waiting in line to get in. As a result, the Westin O'Hare had been calling American Airlines and begging them to release this block of rooms so they could rent them out at full price. But American Airlines refused to do so until all their inconvenienced passengers were taken care of.

I'm not the only passenger with a story like this about American Airlines; shortly after this incident, American went on to become the largest airline in the free world. You can't accomplish a feat like this if your customers aren't talking about you and saying great things. I bet in the last several years, I've told more than 10,000 people about this incident. I'm probably one of American Airlines' best salespeople and they don't pay me one cent in commission or bonus. They just keep on giving me the same high-quality service I've grown to expect, especially in those situations where I am inconvenienced.

Skeptics are quick to point out that there is a cost associated with all this, and there is, but there is also a tremendous payoff. One recent study pointed out that it costs *five* times more to go out and get a new customer than it does to *maintain* a customer you already have. Furthermore, over time, these well-maintained customers tend to tell others and bring their friends with them at no extra cost.

The second aspect of maintaining an agreement is critical for getting other people to stand in line just for the privilege of doing you a favor. The key here is that when someone goes the extra mile to do something nice for you, you make sure that you make this person feel so good about what they have just done that they can't wait for a chance to do something nice for you again.

I have my cars fixed by an establishment called Don's Repair. I was *referred* to this place several years ago by my brother. Although this place was a little out of the way for me, my brother assured me Don's prices were good and when Don fixed something, it stayed fixed. Well, I must admit that Don not only lived up to his advance billing, he was also a nice guy. So I started referring some of my friends to Don. They were also impressed with the quality of Don's service and began referring their friends. As a result, Don's business began to grow rather nicely.

One day, I was driving around town when my car started making a chugging sound and began to lose power. Gently, I nursed my car over to Don's Repair. It was a very busy day and I could see when I arrived that he had a lot of work backed up. However, when Don saw me get out of my car, he immediately dropped what he was doing and came over to see what I needed. I raised the hood and started the car so Don could hear the chugging noise. After listening for about fifteen seconds, Don informed me that I had a disconnected hose and that my carburetor was sucking air. He reached down and reconnected the hose to the carburetor. Sure enough, the chugging noise went away. Don, however, burned his hand slightly on my hot engine during the process. Then he put a clamp on the hose so it wouldn't pull off again in the future.

The whole process took about ten minutes of Don's

time. As he slammed down my hood, I pulled out my checkbook and asked Don what the charge was. Don told me that as I was a regular customer, and it really hadn't taken him very long, there would be no charge. I argued that his time and inconvenience had to be worth something and reminded him that he did put one of his clamps on my hose. At this point Don looked up at me and said, "You don't understand, do you?" Being somewhat puzzled, I said, "Understand what?" Don answered, "You are the cheapest advertising I can buy. I know what you are going to do when you leave here—you're going to tell your friends, and *that* is what makes my business grow!"

Don was right. He knew exactly what he was doing. To this day, I carry around a stack of Don's business cards in my briefcase. And when anyone asks me if I know a good place where they can get their car repaired, the first thing I do is hand them one of Don's business cards. Then I spend a few minutes telling them how great it is to do business with Don. I function as one of Don's best salespeople and I sell Don very actively. I get him lots of new business, and I don't cost Don one cent!

I get the feeling that I'm not the only unpaid salesperson working for Don. During the last three years, Don's business has grown 600 percent and he has never advertised. It's strictly word of mouth on the part of excited and satisfied customers. Doing business in this manner has also produced an interesting side benefit for Don. He almost never gets stuck with a bad check, because everyone who does business with him is a trusted friend.

### Maintaining the Relationship

In addition to maintaining the agreement, it is also necessary to maintain the relationship. If you don't maintain relationships, they begin to deteriorate and the level of trust falls off. Once the trust is gone, there is no possibility for genuine commitment. People don't commit to people they don't trust nor do they stand in line to do them favors.

Maintain a relationship the same way you start one: Spend some time visiting with the same people you deal with without asking them for anything. If the only time you visit these people is when you want something, you become known to them as a moocher, user, or taker. Eventually, these people will no longer look forward to your coming and they will take their business elsewhere.

I have an eleven-year-old son named Philip. If we have spent time together and feel good about each other, and I ask Philip to mow the lawn, chances are he will agree. On the other hand, if I have been gone for a week and we haven't seen each other, much less done anything together, and then I ask Philip, in that same loving tone of voice, to mow the lawn, the answer will probably be some form of no. He is saying to me, "Dad, you don't care about me. If you did, you would have been here. All you care about is some cheap form of slave labor to get your grass cut!"

Several years ago, Philip came home from school on a Thursday afternoon. As he walked in, my wife and I asked him the usual questions about his day like, "How was school? Did you have fun today? What did you learn?" Philip's response was to shrug his shoulders and walk into his room. My wife then turned to me and remarked that something was wrong between us and Philip. I agreed with her.

After looking at the PRAM Model for several minutes, I proclaimed that it was very definitely a maintenance problem. I suggested that we needed to get into Philip's world and convince him that we were not the enemy. At this point, we could hear Philip in his room playing with his toy cars.

Off to Philip's room we went. We got down on the floor with Philip, grabbed a handful of toy cars, and proceeded to make automobile noises right along with him. I have to admit that Philip was a little bewildered at first; the first thing out of his mouth was "What are you doing?" We told him we just wanted to play with him for a while. My wife and I stayed in Philip's room playing with him for forty-five minutes and all three of us really had a good time. And for the next few days Philip never stopped talking about what was going on his life.

My wife and I were thrilled. We could actually say that the relationships between us and Philip couldn't be better. The trap that most of us fall into when we develop such a relationship, however, is to think it will remain at a high level with no additional effort on our parts. Nothing could be further from the truth. Doing so is what's commonly referred to as taking people for granted. If my wife and I had failed to maintain our relationship with Philip for a week, we would have been right back where we started, if not further back.

Maintaining a relationship is a continuous process. Relationships are living arrangements between people and they have to be regularly fed if they are to remain alive. As one woman so eloquently put it at one of my seminars, "What you're really saying by telling us that relationship maintenance is a continuous process is that you never ever really have it made, do you?" This is especially true when it comes to dealing with customers. The minute you take them for granted, they start looking for another place to take their business.

## Maintaining the Plan

The way you maintain a plan is simply by listening to the people you have been dealing with. If you listen long enough and hard enough to these people, they will tell you exactly what it's going to take to motivate them to give you what you'll want the next time around.

As logical and easy as this sounds, most people are reluctant to do it. Most people don't like to listen to their customers. As Tom Peters said, "We've developed a contempt for customers!" We don't like listening to what they have to say because the only time they say anything is when they tell us what they don't like about our products or services. They're usually angry and venting hostility.

Still, we must force ourselves to listen and listen hard because ideas for new products and services come to us via customer complaints about our current product or service.

One very smart car dealer in Madison, Wisconsin, epitomizes the active listening process and his efforts landed him on the front page of *The Wall Street Journal*. This dealer offered free cab service to and from work to customers who would drop their cars off in the morning to get them serviced or repaired. Offering such a service was a gesture that in and of itself caused him to get noticed. But the car dealer's efforts went beyond this. Every six months this car dealer would give dinner parties for the cab drivers involved. At these dinners, he would ask them what his customers were saying about him, his employees, and the way he ran his business. As the car dealer remarked in the article written about him, "If they won't tell a cab driver what's bothering them, who will they tell?" He went on to say that gathering this important information allowed him to stay in touch with his customers and one step ahead of his competition.

At this point, we've taken the Win-Win Negotiation process full circle. If we actively stay tuned to our customers, the planning step is virtually done for the next go-around.

## APPLYING THE PRAM MODEL TO SELLING

The next four chapters focus on the how-to's of each of the four steps of the PRAM Model as they relate to successful selling. I have renamed these four steps with titles that are oriented less toward negotiation in general and oriented more toward the selling process. I renamed planning "Planning for Positive Results" in order to communicate that planning, as a selling activity, is meaningless unless it zeros in on the accomplishment of clearly defined results. Relationships are covered in "Avoiding NO," because the easiest

thing for a prospective customer to tell you is no, and that's
what you'll get if you ask for anything before you've built
your relationship. Once no has been successfully avoided, it
is then possible to "Get to YES," the new name for reaching
an agreement. You can only get to yes once you have successfully avoided no. The final step of the PRAM Model
was renamed "Turning Your Customers into a Sales Force."
Successful salespeople make their living from repeat business and referrals. This is the step where you mobilize your
customers and manage them as your own personal sales
force.

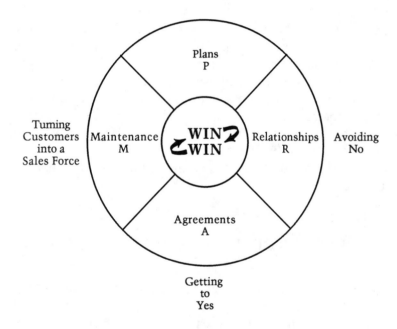

THE PRAM MODEL
APPLIED TO SELLING

# CHAPTER FOUR

# Planning for Positive Results

SEVERAL YEARS AGO, I had the opportunity to listen to a speech given by the vice-president of marketing for a large food manufacturing and distribution company. As he talked about his company's retail cookie division, he pointed out that this segment of the company had lost money for the last three years in a row. I remember thinking to myself that this person was definitely not planning for positive results. It was more like he was planning for negative results and hoping to make it up in volume! It also occurred to me that probably no one in their right mind would go into the cookie business under such circumstances.

Wally "Famous" Amos, founder of the Famous Amos Chocolate Chip Cookie Corporation, decided to plan for *positive* results under this same set of circumstances. He concluded that there was big money to be made by manufacturing and selling cookies if he did things right. He determined that if he presented the prospective customer with a cookie that tasted even better than the ones Mother used to make he could charge premium prices and still sell all the cookies he could produce. Planning for positive results allowed Wally Amos to take this country by storm with his chocolate chip cookies. In fact, his success as a cookie entrepreneur was so phenomenal that he was featured on the cover of *Time* magazine. Not only did his customers not complain about those premium prices, they were happy to pay them!

As important as it is, planning is one of those activities for which people have a love-hate feeling. Most people agree planning is an activity essential to the success of just about anything. On the other hand, many of these same people see planning as an unpleasant task that they would just as soon not have to bother with. When it comes to selling, most people would rather sell than plan. This is one of the key reasons why most people who sell things aren't as successful as they would like to be.

Planning can be viewed as an exciting and worthwhile activity, but only when the results you are trying to achieve are brought clearly into focus. The specific steps of the planning process are discussed below.

## CLARIFY THE RESULTS TO BE ACHIEVED

As trite as it might sound, it is this activity that focuses and crystallizes the rest of the planning process. If you don't have a firm grip on what you want to accomplish and what you are going to sell to achieve your desired results, planning is a meaningless activity. On the other hand, once this phase of the planning process is completed, the rest falls into place. Once Tom Monahan (owner of Domino's Pizza) decided he wanted to become a millionaire by making and selling pizza, it quickly became clear that each million dollars along the way would require a certain number of stores, each achieving a certain level of profitability.

If you want to make $250,000 a year as a dentist, it's going to take a certain number of patients each paying you a certain amount of money per year. If you want to become your company's top salesperson, this might mean adding a certain number of new customers, while at the same time continuing to do business with your current customers.

## IDENTIFY THE PEOPLE WHO STAND BETWEEN YOU AND SUCCESS

Those who stand between you and success (or failure) are the people you need to take through all four steps of the PRAM Model. These are the people you need to have standing in line just waiting for the chance to do you a favor. Although the need for this activity might seem obvious, my consulting experience has shown me that most people do not do it very well.

For example, I have consulted for one of the Big Eight accounting firms. On one occasion, I was dealing with the division that provided accounting services to growing businesses that were, for the most part, managed by the entrepreneur who founded the business. The management of this division was very proud of a study they had completed that contained a detailed profile of their target customers (i.e., entrepreneurs). They knew what these entrepreneurs had for breakfast, what kind of cars they were likely to drive, the type of spouse they were likely to marry, and so forth. As one of this division's top executives put it, "We know our target customers inside out and now we're going after them."

At this point, I was shown the marketing plan this division's management had developed to go after their target customers. I must admit that it was an impressive document. It looked well researched, read logically, and contained some fascinating bells and whistles. For a few moments, I was somewhat dazzled.

Then I asked the division manager where most of his new business was currently coming from. He informed me that much of it came as the result of *referrals* from bankers and attorneys. The reason was that an entrepreneur starting a business usually needed the services of a banker and an attorney long before he needed the services of a public accounting firm. Most entrepreneurs obtain their accounting services from local bookkeeping firms or independent accountants when their business is first starting out. However, as these businesses grow, they eventually reach a point where a local bookkeeping firm or independent accountant can no longer adequately supply the required accounting services. At this point, the entrepreneur realizes he or she needs to utilize the services of a public accounting firm, and asks his or her banker or attorney (people whom he or she has come to trust) to recommend one of the Big Eight accounting firms. "Fortunately," the manager said, "some of these bankers and attorneys just happened to recommend our firm." The conversation that followed between the division manager and me went something like this:

I asked the division manager, "What percentage of your new business comes to your firm as the result of such referrals?"

"At least 70 percent," he replied.

"Then why don't I find bankers and attorneys in your marketing plan?" I inquired.

"Oh, they wouldn't be in our marketing plan," replied the division manager, "because they're not customers."

I asked, "Why don't you consider bankers and attorneys customers?"

"Because they don't spend any money with our firm," was the division manager's response.

I was flabbergasted and with great vigor I asked, "Are you saying that a group of people that is responsible for more than 70 percent of your growth shouldn't be in your marketing plan?" I went on, "These people may not be customers in the traditional sense, but they definitely stand between you and success or failure. These are the people you need to take through the PRAM Model, because these are the people you need to have standing in line just waiting for a chance to do you a favor!"

The division manager was shocked at what he had just learned and immediately made the decision to include bankers and attorneys in his division's marketing plan.

Another of my clients had a similar problem identifying those people who stood between the company and failure. This particular company had education centers all over North America in which they taught various types of technical courses to high school graduates.

This company had a fair number of salespeople whose job it was to sell these technical courses, which sold for about $9,000 each at the time, to people who had graduated from high school or who were about to graduate from high school. Each year, the top 5 percent of their sales force (those who generated the most dollars) were rewarded with a week-long trip to Maui for them and their spouses. My job was to go to Maui and pump up these "5 percenters" and show them what they needed to do in order to be a 5 percenter the following year.

About a month before the program, I was paid a visit by the vice-president of sales for this company. Several days prior to our meeting, he had watched a videotape of me making a similar type of presentation to another group. This vice-president kicked off the meeting by saying, "Ross, I watched your presentation and I have some real problems with it." Needless to say, I was stunned as well as crushed by his comment.

He went on, "In your presentation, you say that if salespersons do their job right, over time, 80 percent of their sales should come from repeat and referral business."

"Absolutely!" I said, "But only if they do their job right."

"Well, I beg to differ with you," he said, "because our situation is unique."

"In what way?" I asked.

The vice-president went on to say, "First of all, we have

*no* repeat business. The reason is that once someone takes our course, he or she is certainly not going to take it again. In other words, all of our sales are one-time sales and we get very few referrals from our students. So keep that in mind when you make your presentation." He also told me the major problem he wanted me to address was that very few of the salespeople who made their way into this elite top 5 percent group attained this achievement from year to year. He speculated that most of these people were so burned out as the result of the effort it took to achieve this lofty goal that it took them a good part of the next year to recover. Consequently, their performance dropped off dramatically. He said that any tools I could give these people to help alleviate this problem would be greatly appreciated.

After we parted company, I was still in somewhat of a state of shock. When he said his salespeople experienced no repeat business and very little in the way of referrals, he had struck a heavy blow at the core of everything I stood for. I sat in the Phoenix airport for quite a while after he left, trying to figure out where my thinking had gone wrong. Then all of a sudden the light went on.

"Ahah!" I thought to myself. "If the only people this vice-president considers to be his company's customers are the high school graduates who are qualified to take the technical courses his company offers, I'll just bet that his company's real customers are people like high school guidance counselors, principals, and other school officials who are in a position to refer these high school graduates to his salespeople. This is where the repeat and referral business comes from, not from the high school graduates themselves."

At this point, I remember smiling victoriously and thinking, "This guy has no clue which side his bread is buttered on and I can't wait to get to Maui."

A month later, when the time for the program finally arrived, I was ready. There were about seventy to eighty people assembled. After some discussion about the PRAM Model and how it works, I finally got to the point in the program where I asked the question, "Who are the people who stand between you salespeople and success or failure?" In other words, I asked them to tell me specifically who their customers were.

Immediately several hands went up and the unanimous answer was, "High school seniors and graduates." I then asked the salespeople to redefine the question from meaning only those people who were qualified to take their courses. I asked them to expand it to also include those people who were in a position to refer qualified high school seniors and graduates to them. Then I asked the group, "Now tell me who your customers are?"

At first the room fell silent and then the hands slowly started to go up. The first answer was, "High school guidance counselors and other school officials." The next person said that he got a number of referrals from people at the Veteran's Administration office. Another person said that he had gotten to know several people at the Employment Security Commission and that this had been a good source of referrals. Someone else related a similar story regarding his experience in dealing with the Salvation Army. And so it went until we had listed more than twenty sources that could refer high school seniors and graduates to these salespeople.

At this point, one of the several people who made this top 5 percent group every year said that referrals from sources like this were the primary reason for her success. She went on to say, "If I had to sell all these courses by myself, I'd burn out long before I got to Maui. But by building and maintaining relationships with people who are in a position to refer my customers to me, I start out the year with 80 percent of my quota already in the bag." She went on to say, "Once someone comes in with a strong referral from a high school or Veteran's Administration counselor, they're already sold. All I have to do is fill out the paperwork."

The vice-president of sales, who had visited me a month earlier in Phoenix, was sitting in the back of the room listening very attentively as this woman made her comments. When she finished, the vice-president looked up at me, smiled, and gave me a very appreciative "thumbs up."

The lesson to be learned here is that when you try to identify those people who stand between you and success or failure, don't just look at the people who spend the money. Rather, take some time trying to find out who actually influences the decision. Often, these people are more important to your success than those you would consider your customers from a traditional standpoint. If you find this to be the case, it's critical to your success that these people be taken through the PRAM process also.

## KNOW WHAT YOU WANT
## FROM THE CUSTOMER

Again, this step might seem obvious, but it's one of those things that many people in selling do *not* do well. Often, the tendency is to look only at this activity from a short-term perspective—to get the order. Successful salespeople, on the other hand, take a much longer-term view of this activity. They not only want the order, they want the *business!*

As we all know, IBM manufactures and sells computers for many different applications. IBM knows exactly what it wants from its customers. Yes, IBM wants them to buy its computers, but what IBM really wants from its customers goes far beyond just making a sale or getting an order. IBM also wants them to come back to IBM as their needs change. IBM looks beyond the initial order from its customers; it is also looking ahead to secure any repeat business that might come from these same customers.

Locking in the initial order and any repeat business, however, is still not enough for IBM. They want even more from their customers. They want their customers to *sell!*

IBM wants its customers to feel so good about having dealt with IBM that these customers feel compelled to tell others to do business with IBM.

Like IBM, all highly successful salespeople take this longer term view of what they want from their customers. That is, they not only want their customers to buy, they want them to keep buying over the long haul, and they want their customers to enthusiastically sell on their behalf. It's the ability to generate referral business that separates the highly successful salespeople from everyone else. If you can secure the referral aspect of the business, you can pretty much assume that the initial order and the repeat business are yours also.

In reality, 25 percent of your success as a salesperson rests with your ability to secure the initial order. The second 25 percent of your success is directly related to your ability to generate repeat business from these same customers. Most important, however, a full 50 percent of your success is tied to your ability to get your customers to refer other customers to you! So, in trying to decide what you want from your customers, make referral business your number one priority.

## ANTICIPATE WHAT THE CUSTOMER WANTS FROM YOU

In order to give a customer those things that are going to motivate him to give you what you want in return, you have to know what his wants and needs are. Unfortunately, research shows that anticipating another person's wants and needs is not something most of us do well. This is especially true when it comes to dealing with customers. There is a tendency on the part of most of us to assume we know what a customer's wants and needs are, rather than to do the legwork necessary to find out what those wants and needs actually are.

This was exactly what happened at Vingresor Airlines in Sweden. The top managers of this firm, most of whom were just over thirty years old, had come to realize that senior citizens were a category of customer worth pursuing in the travel business. In their infinite wisdom, this top management team assumed that Swedish senior citizens were fearful of traveling abroad and would want to stay in special hotels filled with other Swedish senior citizens. They also assumed that older people preferred getting out and seeing the sights, as opposed to sunbathing on the beaches. So they arranged lots of brief excursions interspersed with plenty of restroom breaks.

The top management at Vingresor never bothered to verify these assumptions. They went ahead and invested $100,000 in brochures alone to promote their tour packages, only to have no one sign up. Subsequent market research revealed the cause of this colossal failure. As it turned out, Swedish senior citizens actually preferred to be mixed in with younger adults in hotels that catered to active lifestyles. In addition, over sight-seeing, they preferred sunbathing in places like Mexico, the Canary Islands, and Sri Lanka.

Often we fail to realize that wants and needs have two dimensions: business and personal. The business dimension deals with the factual aspects of a sale—things like price, quality, level of service, and so on. The personal dimension deals with the human aspects of a business transaction. Any highly successful salesperson will tell you that while both dimensions are important, paying attention to the personal aspect of a sale is what really makes the difference.

A number of years ago, shortly after I completed my Ph.D., I decided I wanted to get into the consulting and training business. I had picked up a few small jobs, but nothing of any great size. Finally, my chance came to land what I considered a biggie. The job involved forty days' worth of training per year for an indefinite number of years. I was excited and started putting a selling strategy together to make sure I landed this job. I *assumed*, as there were lots of good consultant/trainers running around, that I was in a very competitive situation and the customer would primarily be interested in price. Thus, I decided I would lower my already low asking price by 25 percent in order to make sure I would have a fighting chance to land this job.

I arrived at the corporate headquarters on a Monday morning at 8:15 to be interviewed and, I hoped, to negotiate the price and terms of an agreement. I was met in the lobby by one of the members of the corporate staff who informed me that the meeting would start a half hour later than originally scheduled. The reason for this was that the corporate staff was supposed to have met the previous Friday to jointly plan the meeting with me. However, the president called them into another meeting, which lasted past 5:30 P.M., and the planning meeting concerning me never took place. This staff member apologized for inconveniencing me and took me to his office where he told me to make myself at home until the meeting started.

As it turned out, this staff person had a secretary who was very friendly and personable. After we had talked for a while, I felt comfortable asking her some questions about the training program. When I asked if her company had ever conducted such a training program in the past, she told me they had during the previous year, but it had ended in disaster. She went on to say that the instructors had done such a poor job that the program participants had gotten up and walked out before noon on the first day of the program. Moreover, she informed me that the corporate staff was really under the gun to find a quality instructor this time, because the president himself was going to sit in on the program to make sure it was done right. She also volunteered that because one of the staff members had attended one of my seminars during the previous year, I was the only person they were considering for the job!

As you can see, my initial assumptions could not have been more wrong. This staff's main concern was not low price; it was whether or not I would make them look good in front of the president. If I could convince them that I would do just that, the job would be mine and price would not even be an issue (as long as it was within reason). I immediately raised my asking price by 50 percent and quickly developed a strategy to convince the corporate staff that I would make them look good in front of the president. I got the job and the price I asked was not even questioned. The president loved the program and I went on to do it for five more years until everyone in the corporation who needed the program had been through it.

## DETERMINE WHAT YOU CAN DO FOR THE CUSTOMER THAT WILL MOTIVATE HIM/HER TO DO WHAT YOU WANT DONE IN RETURN

This final step of the planning process requires you to effectively integrate the information you have gathered during the previous four steps. To successfully execute this step, you must be clear on the results you want to achieve, you must have identified who stands between you and success or failure, you must know specifically what you want from those people, and what they want from you. Once you have this information, provided it's correct, then those things that you need to do for the customer in order to motivate him to do what you want done in return become obvious.

For example, as mentioned earlier, IBM knows exactly what it wants from its customers. IBM wants its customers to buy computers, to keep buying them, and to refer new customers to IBM. IBM also knows what its customers want from IBM. IBM's customers don't normally want the world's best computer. In fact, most of these customers would be hard-pressed to explain what the world's best computer is. What these customers do want is a computer that will take care of their needs in a very satisfactory manner. And, more important than the computer itself, these customers place a high value on service. They like knowing that if anything breaks down or goes wrong, IBM will take care of the situation in very short order. Knowing this, IBM provides its customers with a computer that is adequate for the customer's needs along with *incredible* service. In return, IBM's customers provide IBM with a high level of repeat and referral business, and are very eager to volunteer positive testimonials and accolades about the benefits of doing business with IBM. What's more, these customers pay premium prices for the privilege of doing business with IBM.

A Mexican restaurant in my neighborhood, called Mi Amigo's, is also a master at planning for positive results. The management realizes that children often have a strong influence on where the family is going to dine—especially during the week. The management also realizes that what really influences the children's decision is not so much the food, although the food has to be acceptable to them, but any special treatment that is directed specifically at them. Thus, when the meal is ended, the management takes some extra steps to make sure that the children remember their dining experience at Mi Amigo's in a very positive way. First, when the waitress brings the check, she also brings a delicious chocolate mint candy for everyone at the table. This is the highlight of the children's evening and they are all smiles. But there's more to come. On the way out, the hostess is holding a large basket filled with suckers and each child is allowed to reach in and choose the exact sucker he or she wants.

As inexpensive and mundane as these little gestures may seem to you, they are incredibly effective. Whenever Mom and Dad are too tired to cook dinner and the decision is made to eat out, the first thing out of our children's mouths is, "Let's go to Mi Amigo's!" I can assure you that these management gestures work on other families besides ours. Whenever you arrive at Mi Amigo's after 6:00 P.M., you can bet there will be a line, but it's a line most kids don't mind waiting in.

# CHAPTER FIVE

## Avoiding No

Avoiding no is probably the most critical aspect of successful selling because the easiest thing for a new prospective customer to tell you is no. The easiest way to avoid no is not to try to sell this prospective customer anything until *after* you've established your relationship with him. The biggest single mistake that people who are new or unsuccessful at selling make is—when they come into contact with a prospective customer—to reel off immediately a list of features and benefits of whatever it is they are selling. In the early stages of the selling process, a prospective customer is less interested in features and benefits and more interested in finding out whether he or she can trust you, the salesperson. By coming on strong, you are telling the customer that you really don't care about him. You are sending the customer a message that your main concern is talking him or her out of his or her money, or whatever else it is that you want. If you come on too strong at first, the prospective customer will probably see you as being manipulative or a con artist, and nobody wants to do business with that kind of person.

This is why Joe Girard said he stood in front of his product as well as behind it. He made sure he sold himself to a prospective customer *before* he attempted to sell him a car. Joe realized that if a prospective customer bought him as a person, then selling a car was simply a matter of working out the details. Joe Girard didn't get into the *Guinness Book of World Records* by selling cars; he got there by selling himself!

The four steps associated with successfully avoiding no are described below.

## RECOGNIZE THE IMPORTANT ROLE RELATIONSHIPS PLAY IN BECOMING A SUCCESSFUL SALESPERSON

Without a doubt, the most difficult challenge I face as a consultant and seminar leader is convincing people that building relationships with prospective customers is serious business! Let's reflect for a moment on some of the more recent presidents of the United States. More specifically, let's take a look at how the presence or absence of relationships between some of these presidents and the key members of the House of Representatives and the Senate helped or hindered their ability to get their proposed legislation passed.

Before Lyndon Johnson became president, he had spent more than twenty-five years in Washington, D.C., both as a representative and a senator. During those twenty-five years, Lyndon Johnson had established personal relationships with virtually all of the influential people in Washington, especially the key members of the House and Senate. As a result, when Lyndon Johnson became president, he had a whole network of relationships already in place to help him get things done. When he wanted to get a piece of legislation passed, instead of relying solely on the merit of the legislation, he called his friends and told them to make sure the legislation passed. Because of this large network of personal relationships with the key members of the House and Senate, Lyndon Johnson was very effective in getting bills through Congress.

In contrast, let's take a look at Jimmy Carter. Unlike Lyndon Johnson, Jimmy Carter did not have a large network of personal relationships in place when he became president. In fact, his network was almost nonexistent. Although Jimmy Carter was a very bright person with some very good ideas, he had no clue as to the important role that relationships played and he spent little time cultivating them. The sad part was that we had a Democratic president with a Democratically controlled House and Senate, yet Carter was ineffective in getting his legislation passed. He never had a chance to sell Congress his ideas, because he didn't take the time to sell himself.

Finally, let's look at Ronald Reagan. Ronald Reagan started out much like Jimmy Carter in that he had very few relationships with members of the House and Senate when he took office as president. The key difference between him and Carter, however, was that somewhere along the way Reagan had learned to appreciate the important role relationships played in becoming a successful president. As a result, during the first eighteen months Ronald Reagan was in office, he didn't try to sell the members of the House and Senate anything. Instead, he spent these first eighteen months developing relationships with these people, especially key ones like Tip O'Neill.

Reagan recognized that there was one place in Washington, for which most people, regardless of political affiliation, would almost kill for an invitation to dinner—the White House! So one by one he invited each of the key members of the House and Senate to the White House for dinner. It's important to note that the conversation at these dinner parties did not involve heavy-duty politics, but was more lighthearted and fun.

Reagan continued having these dinner parties, and when he felt his relationships with the right people were well enough established, he then began to propose legislation. Almost all of it passed. In fact, Ronald Reagan went on to eclipse Lyndon Johnson as one of the most effective presidents in history in getting his proposed legislation passed. The reason he was so successful was that he developed personal relationships with the people who stood between him and success or failure *before* he tried to sell them anything.

As Tip O'Neill said in *Man of the House*, "Some House members said they saw more of him [Ronald Reagan] during his first four months in office than they saw of Jimmy Carter during his entire four years. . . . Reagan took Congress very seriously and was always coming over to the Capitol for meetings. According to what I heard, he instructed his people, 'Tell me who you want me to call and I'll take care of it.' I would have given my right arm to hear those words from Jimmy Carter." Like Joe Girard, Ronald Reagan did not become such a successful president by selling his ideas; he did it by selling himself.

Achieving success in a big way is something you can't do by yourself. You have to enlist the active support of those people who stand between you and success or failure. And the only way you can enlist these people's active support is to turn them into friends or allies by establishing personal relationships with them that are built on mutual trust.

## PLAN SITUATIONS THAT ALLOW A RELATIONSHIP TO DEVELOP

Schedule some activities that will allow you the chance to get to know the person you are about to deal with and, at the same time, allow this person to get to know you. Activities such as lunches, dinners, golf, or parties afford very good opportunities for developing relationships. Or, if a person is coming from out of town to discuss business with you, consider picking him or her up at the airport. This will favorably impress your out-of-town visitor, because he or she won't be used to such courtesy. In addition, during the course of driving this person to his or her hotel you have a chance to engage in casual conversation and get to know each other.

The key is to schedule activities that allow casual conversation. Trust relationships are not initiated by intense discussions on sensitive business or political issues. Rather, they are initiated by casual conversation about things like the weather, places you've visited, movies, or baseball scores. The time to discuss more serious or sensitive issues is *after* you feel reasonably comfortable with each other.

Several years ago, I was asked to speak at a top management meeting for a large construction firm. There were about twenty people in attendance. After I had spoken for about forty minutes, I couldn't help detecting a fair amount of tension within this group. At first, I couldn't put my finger on where this tension was coming from. Then I noticed that all the older managers were sitting on one side of the room while all the younger managers were sitting on the other side. Having been brought to this meeting to help identify and solve problems, I suggested that the two groups might be harboring a little animosity toward each other. When the room fell deadly silent, I knew I was onto something. Since no one was talking, I suggested that maybe the younger managers resented the fact that the older managers were reluctant to turn any of the control of the firm over to them, and the older managers resented the younger managers' attempting to take some of the control away from them. I went on to point out that the two groups of managers probably didn't feel comfortable with each other and hence didn't trust each other.

At this point, representatives from both groups acknowledged that this was true and that the problem had been brewing for some time. To make matters worse, when the older managers had parties, they didn't invite the younger managers and vice versa. The only time members of the two groups interacted was during the conduct of their jobs. This wasn't the proper environment to get these relationships back on track.

Since we were all at a very nice resort for a three-day period, I suggested that they engage in some sort of activity where the members of the two groups could spend some time with each other on a one-on-one basis, such as golf. I suggested that this be organized so that each golf cart contained one person from the older group and one person from the younger group.

At this point, one of the older managers expressed his dissatisfaction with my idea. He emphatically pointed out that the younger managers were better golfers and would make the older managers look sick! I assured this older manager that I appreciated his point, but that my only suggestion was that these two parties go golfing together in an attempt to get to know each other. I never suggested that they keep score. I then suggested that pairing up in the golf carts and riding around town for three or four hours might be an alternative, since the purpose of this activity was merely to provide an opportunity for the members of the two groups to get to know each other better.

The next day these two groups of managers played golf. At a cocktail party that evening, I could already notice a change in the atmosphere. That was several years ago. Today these two groups still play golf together on a regular basis. The animosity between them has disappeared and has been replaced by teamwork.

This example points out several things about relationship-building activities. First, these activities have to be noncompetitive. Competition is not conducive to fostering trust. Second, relationship-building activities should provide ample opportunities for casual conversation—conversation where the person can be himself or herself, talk about whatever comes up, and not be rushed.

Finally, relationship-building activities should be enjoyable and even fun. This brings out the best in people, which is obviously conducive to fostering a trusting relationship.

## CULTIVATING THE RELATIONSHIP

Fortunately, cultivating personal relationships is something at which all of us have at least some experience. Most of us have developed relationships with childhood friends, schoolmates, and co-workers, as well as our neighbors, spouses, and children. Of course, some people seem to enjoy developing relationships with new people, while others have a hard time developing them and avoid such opportunities whenever possible.

Unfortunately, a desire to avoid developing relationships does not change the critical role that relationships play in achieving a high level of success. You simply have to develop them, lots of them, if you want to be a successful salesperson. The goal of this section is to take the mystery out of the process of developing relationships so that even the most timid of people can feel comfortable and eventually become quite proficient at it. And for those of you who feel you've already mastered the process, the pages that follow also contain some ideas that will help you become even better at it.

## THE THREE PHASES OF A RELATIONSHIP

As a relationship evolves, it passes through three distinct phases: liking, bonding, and trusting. In cultivating a relationship, it is important to recognize this natural order. A relationship is something that simply cannot be forced or rushed; it must be allowed to evolve naturally. All too often, people dive into the process and immediately start trying to convince the other person that they should trust them. This approach generally doesn't work—your trust-worthiness is not something of which you can convince another person with words. Rather, trust can only evolve *after* the liking and bonding phases have occurred.

## Liking

During your initial encounter with another person, the extent to which you like or dislike this person is generally based on bias rather than facts. If a stranger were to walk into a room where you were standing, your initial reaction might be based upon such things as the clothes this person was wearing, how attractive this person looked, or whether this person appeared to espouse values or interests similar to yours. If this stranger took the trouble to come over and pay you a compliment, you might be inclined to feel very positive about this person.

Although first impressions are very superficial, based on bias, and just as often wrong as right, as the old adages tell us, "People tend to judge a book by its cover," and "You only get one chance to make a first impression." Thus, it's a good idea to take the necessary steps to make a positive first impression. Dress appropriately, be well groomed, and make sure you have something positive to say.

On the other hand, these old adages make creating a favorable first impression seem far more important than it really is. Although it's to your advantage to get the relation-ship off on the right foot, we're talking about developing a long-term relationship. No matter how favorable a first impression you make, eventually you are going to have to provide more substantive reasons why this other person should continue to like you and want to pursue the rela-tionship further. With each subsequent encounter, the at-traction between you and the person you're dealing with becomes based less upon bias and more upon mutual inter-ests and concerns.

How do you go about getting someone else to like you

or feel good about you? The answer is quite simple. First, you must recognize that, without exception, all the people you deal with have basically the same psychological makeup and needs. They are all sensitive, have delicate egos, and have an insatiable desire to feel good about themselves. So be sensitive toward these people and demonstrate that you genuinely are one of those rare people who care as much about other people as you do about yourself. Be a good and sincere listener and recognize that people absolutely love to talk about themselves and things that are important to them, such as their work, their accomplishments, their interests, or their families. Try to put yourself in other people's shoes and see the world from their point of view. Feel their problems as they feel them. As the authors of the book *Non-Manipulative Selling* put it so well, "People buy services or products most often because they feel that they and their problems are understood by the seller—not because the buyer is made to understand the product by an insistent salesperson."

So don't try to fake that perfect first impression or any other aspect of the relationship. Rather, let that first impression be a true projection of the real you, the person who really cares. Then the other person won't be let down as they get to know you better; instead, he or she will be impressed that you actually are what you initially appeared to be. The bottom line to all this was simply and correctly stated by Bob Cialdini in his excellent book *Influence: How and Why People Agree to Things* when he said that "as a rule, we most prefer to say yes to the requests of people we know and like."

## Bonding

Bonding involves the discovery of common interests and experiences. I live in Arizona and whenever I come across someone whom I initially like and want to get to know better, the first question I normally ask is, "Are you originally from Arizona?" I know full well the answer is probably no, because almost everyone who lives in Arizona is from somewhere else. A no gives us something in common because I'm originally from somewhere else also.

The next question I ask is, "Where are you from originally?," knowing there is a 75 percent chance this person is from the Midwest. This gives us another bond because that's where I'm from. My next question is, "Where in the Midwest?" If this person says Chicago or Michigan, we can really get into some serious bonding, because I'm originally from that part of Michigan that is directly across Lake Michigan from Chicago.

Bonding is a process that we all do naturally. The important thing to realize here is that talking to someone about mutual interests and experiences, especially if this person stands between you and success or failure, is not a waste of time. Bonding is absolutely necessary if you ever expect to develop a mutual feeling of trust.

You'll find that some bonds are stronger than others. Obviously, if you were a prisoner of war and you discover that the person you're talking to was also a prisoner of war, this is a much stronger bond than if you discover that you have both read the same book or seen the same movie. But no matter how strong the bond between you and another person, *the bond should never serve as a substitute for trust.* Just because someone is a relative, belongs to the same church or organization, or has shared a meaningful experience with you, there is no reason to assume that this person has your best interests at heart.

I was recently a guest on a radio talk show and a listener called in to share with me such an experience. This person was a World War II navy veteran who had retired in Arizona. Eighteen months prior, he had received a phone call from an old navy buddy, someone he hadn't seen in thirty-five years. The buddy was from Tucson and asked the caller and his wife to come visit them for a weekend so they could catch up on old times. So they got together and during the course of the weekend, this man's buddy told him of a cattle venture he was putting together on his cattle ranch, located in a semi-remote area of Arizona. The venture sounded so attractive that our friend bought in to the tune of $35,000. It never even occurred to him that his old navy buddy might be lying to him. Well, when tax time came and no annual statement arrived, this man called his buddy. The buddy assured him that things were going well, so well, in fact, that he was behind in getting statements out. The caller then filed for a tax extension and waited another month. However, when he called his buddy this time, the phone was disconnected. When he drove out to the site where the ranch was supposed to be, he found nothing but rocks, boulders, and an occasional cactus.

The lesson to be learned from the above example is that bonding merely sets the stage for the final phase in the process, which is the development of mutual trust.


### Trusting

Trusting is based less upon what you say and more upon what you do or fail to do. By jumping the gun and trying to sell another person something before he or she feels comfortable with you or is otherwise ready to buy, you send this person a clear message that you are more concerned with money or whatever else you might be after than you are with his or her welfare.

I had a financial planner call on me several years ago. He came to me with excellent references from several trusted friends, so I gave him the benefit of the doubt. His first comment after some initial chitchat was, "I'm not here to sell you anything."

I remember thinking to myself at the time, "What a refreshing approach."

The gentleman went on to say that what he really wanted to do was to get a feel for some of my personal financial goals. He would then look at these goals, compare them to where I stood at the present, and then run this information through his computer. At our next meeting, he would present me with some options regarding things I could do to make sure I achieved those financial goals.

When this person returned for our second meeting, we spent a great deal of time getting to know each other better. As it turned out, we had some mutual friends, some common interests, and pretty much saw the world from the same perspective. I was starting to really like this person. He then showed me the results of his computer analysis, which among other things revealed a gaping hole in my financial provisions for my family if I were to die suddenly. He pointed out that the situation could be remedied, at least temporarily, with a $100,000 term insurance policy. He then went on to tell me about Individual Retirement Accounts, Self-Employed Pension Plans, and all sorts of things that I, as a person who was getting ready to go into business for myself, ought to know.

Well, I felt so good about this person and what he was telling me that I suggested we meet again the following week when my partner was coming to town, because I knew my partner would be every bit as interested as I. Notice here who is asking for the appointment—not the salesperson, but an excited prospective buyer. This man wasn't trying to sell me; he was simply letting me buy.

At this point, I was happily saying to myself, "I have finally met a salesperson I can trust; a salesperson who really has my best interests at heart." Shortly after, however, the reality of the situation came crashing down around me. As this person was packing up his briefcase, he said to me, "By the way, I've already got the paperwork filled out for this $100,000 term insurance policy. Why don't you just sign it, and we'll get the ball rolling."

When I heard that statement I was stunned. This person had spent the better part of two rather lengthy meetings doing a very good job of convincing me that I could trust him and with one sentence (which probably had been an afterthought), he told me he was more interested in my money than he was in me. The bottom line was, I no longer felt I could trust him. After he left, I called his office and canceled our next appointment and I never saw this person again. Had he not jumped the gun and tried to sell me before I was ready, both my partner and I would have spent a fair amount of money with him.

For a long time afterward, this incident bothered me. I felt cheated and betrayed and annoyed. Finally, several years later, a participant in one of my seminars told me not to take the incident so personally, because this person wasn't intentionally trying to hurt me, he was only doing what he had been taught in school. This is a sad indictment of the quality of sales education and training in this country.

The important thing to keep in mind is that anytime you demonstrate that your interests are more important than the other person's, you run the risk of either violating the trust that already exists or preventing it from developing in the first place. On the other hand, by showing those you deal with that you really do care about their welfare, you are paving the way for a long-term relationship. For example, a friend of mine, who is a purchasing manager, set the stage for a lifelong relationship by showing a salesperson who was visiting from out of town that he cared. The salesperson arrived on a Sunday evening for an all-day meeting on Monday. Shortly after the meeting began, the purchasing manager noticed that the salesperson was wearing a membership pin from Rotary International. Knowing that Rotary met at noon on Mondays and that attendance at meetings was very important to Rotary members, the purchasing manager offered to take the salesperson over to the meeting that day. The salesperson was both surprised and impressed with the purchasing manager's concern for him. As a result of this gesture, the meeting was far more productive than either person had anticipated, which in turn led to their doing business with each other for many years to come. As an old adage puts it, "People don't care how much you know until they know how much you care."

## THE ROLE OF SOCIALIZING

What allows the relationship to progress from liking to trusting? The answer to this question is something you won't find in any sales, marketing, or other business-related book. The process is one that we all engage in every day of our lives with the people we come into contact with. It's commonly referred to as socializing: casual, personal conversations. You have to bring the personal element into these conversations because trust is a personal concept. You can only build trust with another person; you can't build it with companies, organizations, or agencies. People do business with people and they prefer to do business with people they know, like, and trust.

For example, if a politician has a scandal in his personal life, others try to come to the rescue by saying, "Don't judge this person by the way he leads his personal life, judge this person by how he stands on the issues." But as logical as this seems, the truth is we don't elect issues to public office, we elect people. If some aspect of a politician's personal life turns voters off, that politician won't be elected.

When I was a professor at Arizona State University, colleagues used to drop by my office occasionally to ask me if I wanted to go to lunch. Although I always appreciated the invitation, I usually turned it down because I was too busy. Later in life, as I got more and more into the business of selling, I found the opposite to be true. I found I couldn't afford *not* to go to lunch, especially with those people who stood between me and success or failure. Lunch provided the opportunity to engage in casual conversations with pro- spective clients where I got to know them better and vice versa. As a general rule, the more socializing I did with pro- spective clients before we got down to business, the easier it was to work out a mutually satisfactory agreement. This, in- cidentally, is why business lunches are still tax deductible.

Many businesses encourage their salespeople to belong

to various social, professional, and civic organizations. The regular meetings and activities of these organizations provide opportunities to meet and socialize with people who might be in a position to enhance your success. At the same time, it is important to keep in mind that your participation in these organizations is only for the purpose of developing relationships. Never try to sell someone something at one of these meetings or activities. If you do, you run the risk of being perceived as a hustler and no one likes to do business with a hustler. Business should be conducted at a separate time and place, after a relationship has been developed.

## THE POWER OF REFERENCES

A reference is basically a statement of qualification from a mutual acquaintance or friend. References affect all phases of a relationship.

First, a reference affects liking because it creates an image of you in the mind of the person you are about to meet. If a reference is positive, the person to whom the reference was given will visualize you in a positive light. The first impression that you will create for this person will probably be positive because this person expects it to be positive.

Second, a reference affects bonding because it is a bond, in that the reference came from a mutual friend or acquaintance. You can start your conversation off by discussing each of your personal experiences with this mutual friend.

Finally, if a trusted friend of the person you are about to meet gives you a glowing referral, you are going to get the benefit of the doubt when it comes to trusting you. This is the reason that most traditional sales training programs and books tell you to push your customers, clients, or patients for the names of friends or acquaintances who might need your product or service. In fact, one traditional sales training program I attended said to never let go of a customer, after you've closed the sale, until he or she gives you the names of five friends.

This is where I differ with most people doing sales training and consulting. Don't insist on referrals. The best way to get them is to *earn* them. And the way you earn them is through what is often referred to as service. Take even better care of your customers, clients, or patients than they expect you to. If you do this, you won't have to work so hard at selling because your satisfied customers are out there doing it for you.

## DON'T GET DOWN TO BUSINESS TOO QUICKLY

I've said it before but it's worth reiterating: *Don't try to rush the process.* If you push for the sale too quickly, the prospect is likely to question your motives, decide he or she can't trust you, and look to do business with someone else. As Spencer Johnson and Larry Wilson said in *The One-Minute Salesperson*, "People hate to be sold, but they love to buy." Your job as a salesperson should be viewed as making it easy for your customers to buy. Don't try to sell them until they are ready. They won't be ready until they feel comfortable with you—so trying to rush the process will only slow things down.

The customer will generally let you know when he or she is ready to buy. For example, if they show a definite interest in your product or service by asking questions or otherwise indicating a desire to proceed, they are probably ready. On the other hand, if the customer backs away or tries to change the subject when you start getting into the specifics of selling your product or service, this probably means he or she isn't comfortable enough to move on. When this happens, don't force your presentation on them. Back off and continue to work on your relationship until the customer lets you know that he or she is ready. At times like this, it's helpful to remember, you're not after this one particular sale or order, you're after the business.

# CHAPTER SIX

# Getting to Yes

ONCE YOU'VE SUCCESSFULLY avoided no by establishing a mutual sense of trust, getting to yes is really not very difficult. It's merely a matter of working out the details. You and your customer have already, in effect, declared that you'd like to do business with each other. There is no need for a hard sell in this step, because the customer is already in the state of mind where he or she wants to buy. As Ron Willingham said in his book, *Integrity Selling*, "People are more apt to say yes when trust and rapport is high than when selling pressure is high!"

If you are expecting this chapter to include a list of persuasion techniques or closing tactics that will help you to manipulate reluctant customers into a position where they feel they have to say yes, you're going to be disappointed. At the heart of the Win-Win selling process are *trust* and *integrity*. This means absolutely *no* manipulation of any kind whatsoever. *The goal of selling, from a Win-Win perspective, is not to close a sale but to keep it open.*

Although the subject of "how to close a sale" is very popular at sales training programs and seminars, closing implies a sense of finality. In other words, once the customer says yes, the game is over and the winner is the salesperson.

A Win-Win salesperson, however, is not just after the order. That salesperson and his or her customer work together in an atmosphere of trust to find a mutually acceptable solution to a common problem, a solution about which both salesperson and customer feel good. Both should be motivated to follow through on their promises, and both should look forward to doing business together in the future. The Phoenix office of Grubb and Ellis, a very large commercial real estate firm, is the most successful office in the corporate network. They have about seventy salespeople, 70 percent of whom earn six-figure commissions and several of whom earn seven-figure commissions. These salespeople don't view their role so much as selling, but as establishing themselves as trusted consultants and advisors to their customers. The trust level is so high between some of these customers and the Grubb and Ellis salespeople that these customers wouldn't think of buying from anyone else. The attitude among these customers is that their trusted consultant at Grubb and Ellis wouldn't be bringing a piece of property to their attention if he or she didn't think it was in the customer's best interest to consider buying or leasing it.

## VERIFY THE CUSTOMER'S WANTS AND NEEDS

During the planning step of the Win-Win selling process, you tried to determine what you could do for your customer that would motivate your customer to give you what you wanted. Your plan was based on a specific set of assumptions concerning where the customer was coming from and what his or her specific wants and needs were. No matter how well intentioned your plan, if it doesn't meet the customer's needs, it will not motivate the customer to give you what you want. Even worse, if you insist on trying to carry out your plan although it does not meet the customer's needs, it can actually turn the customer off, which could have negative implications for any future business.

A case in point is IBM. In the mid 1980s, the company registered a profit decline for three consecutive years. For a while, company officials were dumbfounded as to the cause. A *Business Week* cover story contained the answer. In that article, IBM's chairman conceded that IBM had simply stopped listening to its customers. Whenever customers came to IBM and asked IBM to design or in some way modify a particular computer so it better fit their needs, IBM tried to sell the customer something that was already on the shelf. The arrogant assumption was that if IBM had developed and produced it, it had to fit the customers' needs. Trying to sell customers equipment that they perceived as not meeting their needs eventually resulted in many of these customers deciding to buy computers from IBM's competitors.

## ASK QUESTIONS AND LISTEN

The way to verify a customer's wants and needs is to ask questions and actively listen to the answers. Your role should be that of a trusted consultant. If you listen long enough, the customer will tell you his or her true wants and needs. This can take some time, as some of these wants and needs will be personal and most people are somewhat reluctant to talk about these, even to trusted friends. Once these true wants and needs are known, and only then, are you in a position to judge the appropriateness of your plan. At this point you can decide if you should stay with your original plan, modify it somewhat, or go back to the drawing board.

I ran into a situation once where I thought I had all the customer's wants and needs nailed down, but they actually changed in midstream. I was competing for a sales training contract for a two-day program with a Health Maintenance Organization. The organization had sent me a detailed set of specifications explaining what I was supposed to include in the program. In my proposal I thoroughly addressed each of these points in detail.

The project was assigned to a staff person who reported directly to the vice-president of operations. While preparing my proposal, I visited this person several times in person and spoke with her many times over the phone. Several weeks after receiving my proposal, she informed me that my proposal clearly stood out as the best and she was going to recommend it for approval to the vice-president.

A week later, she called and told me we needed to discuss my fee—it was too high. This surprised me, because when she essentially told me I had the job in the bag, my fee was never mentioned. As this seemed to be a sensitive issue, I set up an appointment to discuss the issue with her in person rather than over the phone. When we got together several days later, I noticed she tried to keep the discussion at arm's length, which was in stark contrast to the laid back and even fun discussions we'd had in the past.

This told me that she wasn't comfortable with what she was doing, for some reason or other, and that I had better engage in some relationship building if I expected to find out why. So I suggested we go to the cafeteria for a cup of coffee. During the walk to and from the cafeteria, we talked about some non-business-related things such as our families and what we had done over the weekend. When we finally returned to her office, she seemed much more relaxed and no longer attempted to keep the discussion at arm's length.

After confirming that she still liked the technical aspects of my proposal, I asked why my fee had suddenly caused a problem. As she now felt comfortable, she decided to level with me. She went on to tell me that although my fee was on the high side, it was still very acceptable, given the results I had promised to deliver. However, the vice-president, to whom she reported, was one of those people who assumed that consultants usually padded their fees, and expected to be chiseled down a bit. She said that if she didn't get me to lower my price at least a bit, her boss would consider her an ineffective negotiator.

After listening to her for a while longer, I concluded that her true need was not necessarily getting me to lower my fee, but looking good in front of her boss. I then told her that I couldn't lower my fee because it was the same fee I charged everyone else. I told her, however, that I had noticed that while her organization's salespeople were going to attend the seminar, none of the sales managers were scheduled to attend. She informed me that they were to stay in the office to handle any emergencies that came up while their salespeople were in training.

I pointed out that if these managers were to be successful in motivating these salespeople to do the things I was going to teach them, they ought to know what these things were. This staff person agreed, but reiterated the need to take care of any possible emergencies. I then suggested that she organize a dinner for the sales managers at the end of the first day of the program. At that dinner I would present an executive summary of what I covered in the program and would pass on some managerial advice on how to keep the salespeople motivated to do the things I was going to teach them. I told her that since I had nothing else to do that evening, there would be no extra charge.

This staff person was elated at the idea. This gave her something to take back to her boss. As a result, I got the job and my fee. Had I not taken the time to ask questions and verify her true needs, there was no way I would ever have gotten the job.

## IMPLEMENT YOUR WIN-WIN PLAN

Once you've verified the customer's true wants and needs and made any necessary adjustments in your original plan, it's time to put this plan into action. Successfully implementing your Win-Win plan requires that you simultaneously do two things: (1) propose to the customer those things you can do for him that will motivate him to do what you want done, and (2) consider those things the customer is proposing to you in an attempt to motivate you to give him what he wants. This is the "give and take." Be sensitive and flexible toward the customer, making sure that you don't do all the talking or all the taking and that you continually zero in on the customer's true wants and needs.

The thing you don't want to do is to deliver a well-rehearsed canned pitch or presentation that extols every conceivable feature and benefit of your product or service. Canned pitches generally come across as just that. They violate trust because they communicate to your customer that you are more concerned with delivering your presentation than you are with his or her welfare. The most successful sales presentations are not the ones where you tell the customer everything you know about your product or service. Rather, they are the ones where you first convince the customer that you genuinely understand their true wants and needs and then show the customer how what you are proposing fulfills those true wants and needs. As the authors of *Non-Manipulative Selling* put it, "Clients buy because the salesperson truly understands and appreciates their business-related problems, not solely because the client understands the salesperson's product or service."

I was recently asked to submit a proposal to develop a sales training program targeted toward the corporate sales officers of a large bank. Although bank officials had spent a great deal of time deciding what they wanted from the program, the specifications were still rather sketchy in spots. In order to get a better feel for what the bank officials were expecting out of this program, I called the director of training for the bank. She was very nice, but not as knowledgeable about the project as I had hoped. She referred me to the vice-president of marketing and sales. The vice-president was very eager to share his expectations for the training program because he was directly involved, and we talked on the phone for more than an hour. He suggested that, to get a better feel for the sales problems facing his corporate sales officers, I make appointments to visit with several of them in person, which I did.

All of this extra legwork gave me a much clearer vision of what the bank officials hoped to accomplish with this training program, and I incorporated all this new knowledge into my proposal. Ten weeks later, I received a phone call from the vice-president of marketing and sales, who informed me that I had gotten the job. With tongue in cheek, I suggested the reason for this was that I was probably the low bidder. In a very serious tone of voice, the vice-president informed me that mine was actually the highest of all the bids he had received. He went on to inform me that I won the job for two basic reasons. First, I was the only consultant who took the time to find out what the actual training needs of the bank's corporate sales officers were. Second, mine was the only proposal that reflected a knowledge and understanding of those true needs.

## ENGAGE IN MUTUAL PROBLEM SOLVING

No matter how well researched and thought out your plan is, it may still take you only part of the way to where you want to go. For example, a customer might say, "I love your proposal and I would enjoy doing business with you, but your price is too high," or "Your price is fair enough, but the level of service you are proposing still falls short of my actual needs," or "I'm sold on your product, but the labor situation at your plant gives me grave concern about your ability to deliver over time." When these kinds of situations occur, it's time to get down to some serious creative problem solving. That is where you and the customer sit down and work together to come up with a solution that satisfies you both, a Win-Win solution.

A friend of mine was attempting to negotiate a contract with a large publisher to publish and distribute a book he had recently completed. The discussion between the two parties was relatively routine until the issue of the author's royalty came up. The author wanted 15 percent of the $15 retail price of the book. The publisher wanted to pay the author 20 percent of the net price it received from sales to bookstores (which usually reflected a 40 to 50 percent discount from the retail price). The author felt that at a royalty of 20 percent of the net sales to bookstores, he was not making enough money to compensate him for all his hard work. The publisher's position was that at a royalty of 15 percent of the retail price, the publisher was absorbing too much risk. The two parties argued back and forth on the relative merits of each other's position, but this got them nowhere.

Eventually, a representative from the publisher suggested that they stop their arguing and channel their energies toward finding a mutually acceptable solution to this royalty issue. The publisher's representative then asked if there was anything that the publisher could offer on some of the other areas of the contract that would allow the author to feel he was getting an acceptable deal on the royalty of 20 percent of net sales to bookstores. As it turned out, the author was also a widely known speaker and spoke to large audiences all over the world more than a hundred times a year. Furthermore, he planned to sell the book at these programs as soon as it was published. Some quick mental arithmetic told him that his potential sales from this venture could be as much as 80,000 to 120,000 copies per year!

The publisher's normal price for books bought by the author for sales at programs was already in the contract at a 40 percent discount or a price of $9.00 per copy. Having completed his mental analysis of the matter, the author proposed that he could live with a royalty of 20 percent of net sales to bookstores if the publisher would agree to negotiate a significantly lower buy back price with the author. The publisher agreed and the price they mutually established was actual cost to the publisher plus 50 percent, or a net price to the author of $2.00 per copy. This agreement not only left both parties feeling very good about the outcome but it enabled the author to increase the revenue he received from his speaking engagements by $560,000 to $840,000 per year. This turned out to be much more than he would have made from the higher royalty rate.

## DON'T OVERLOOK THE CUSTOMER'S EGO

As simple and logical as mutual problem solving sounds, it's not always easy to do. Egos can sometimes get in the way. It's important to realize that the agreements you reach must effectively satisfy the customer's personal as well as business needs.

One of the most common mistakes that salespeople make is to pay too much attention to the customer's business needs and not enough attention to his personal or ego needs. As Frank Bacon and Tom Butler point out in their book, *Planned Innovation*, when people decide to buy something, 80 percent of the decision is based on emotional factors and only 20 percent is based on rational factors. Yet the vast majority of salespeople persist in spending 80 percent or more of their time on rational reasoning and less than 20 percent of their time on the emotional aspects of the buying decision.

Below are some emotional factors that can assist you

in making sure your customer's ego needs are taken care of. More important than anything on this list, however, is your awareness that taking care of these needs is serious business, if you want to turn your customers into a sales force.

*Allow the Customer Equal Participation in the Mutual Problem-Solving Process.* Don't try to ramrod your ideas through. The problem-solving process must be mutual; otherwise the customer will resist you purely on the basis of ego reasons. Agreeing with you can't be perceived as giving in by the customer. As the authors of *Non-Manipulative Selling* put it, "If you impose solutions upon clients, they will resent both you and your solution."

*Sit Together on the Same Side of the Desk.* This is an idea that Roger Fisher and William Ury presented in *Getting to Yes.* Facing each other during problem-solving discussions creates a confrontational atmosphere. However, when the customer and seller sit next to each other and put the problem in front of them, this signifies a sense of mutual ownership of the problem, and thus promotes an atmosphere of teamwork. Try it during your next selling opportunity; you'll be surprised at how sitting side by side changes the atmosphere.

*Don't Take Your Frustrations Out on the Customer.* At times, the process of searching for the solution that is going to make both buyer and seller happy can be very frustrating. You may encounter a situation in which every time you propose what you think is a valid solution to a problem, the customer tells you why it won't work. Your emotions begin to build and pretty soon you are tempted to vent them on the customer. If you do so, the customer will take it personally and will probably react in kind. If you are going to vent any frustration, make sure you direct it at the problem and not at the customer. Make sure that any communication that *is* directed at the customer is positive in nature and supports his ego. As Fisher and Ury said in *Getting to Yes*, "Be hard on the problem, but soft on the people."

*Don't Overreact to Emotional Outbursts.* There are going to be times when the customer becomes frustrated and decides to vent his frustrations on you. When this occurs, don't even think of attacking back; that would only add fuel to the fire and halt any progress toward reaching an agreement. Instead, try to keep in mind that the customer isn't necessarily upset or angry at you personally, but is probably frustrated with the situation. The rule of thumb to be applied to situations like this is to "kill the customer with kindness." If the customer wants to vent, let him vent, and don't take it personally. Sometimes, simply acknowledging the situation with a comment like "Obviously you are frustrated, let's talk about it" can go a long way toward calming the situation. In other cases, changing the scenery by taking a break, getting a cup of coffee, or going to lunch can help defuse the situation and get the process of reaching an agreement back on track.

## FINALIZING THE AGREEMENT

This is the shortest section in this chapter, because once you and the customer have worked out acceptable solutions to problems, the customer has essentially said yes. All that remains to be done at this point is to make sure there are no misunderstandings regarding the agreement and to put in writing those things that might cause future misunderstandings. The best way to avoid misunderstandings is to spend some time talking over the agreement with the customer after it has been reached. The reason for this discussion is to make sure that you and the customer both feel that all relevant issues and problems have been solved in a

Win-Win manner and that you both are absolutely certain about what you have agreed.

At this point, you and the customer might want to ask yourselves this question: "If anything is going to go wrong, where is it likely to occur and, if it does occur, how are we going to resolve it?" In this manner, you're putting in place a system to resolve these potential problems before they occur. In the event something does go wrong, you and the customer can get on to the business of resolving the problem rather than spending your time arguing over whose fault it is. For example, let's assume that you are a manufacturer's representative and represent a number of different firms. Once the customer places the order with you, you turn it over to the appropriate company to fill the order. The question that the customer might have is who should he call in the event the order doesn't arrive on time. Should he call the factory directly or should he call you? Such issues can become very sticky once a problem does occur, and can undermine even a long-term trust relationship. The best time to deal with such issues is right now, while you're still in each other's presence and the agreement is still fresh in your mind.

You may have noticed that the word *close* does not appear in this chapter except to inform you that closing has no place in the Win-Win selling process. The very idea of closing a sale implies that once the customer says yes, it's all over. Although this may be true for those short-sighted salespeople who view their job as solely that of getting a one-time order from a customer, it is not true for those of us who look to our customers as a source of repeat and referral business. Remember: Our goal is not to close the sale, but to keep it open.

# CHAPTER SEVEN

# Turning Your Customers into a Sales Force

YOU ARE NOW positioned to turn your customers into a sales force. This all-important result depends on effectively performing the maintenance aspect of Win-Win selling. You must maintain three things with each of your customers: the agreement, the relationship, and the plan. Maintenance is the secret of highly successful salespeople. If you ever observe these people, you will notice that they have reached the point where they are no longer doing very much direct selling to the customer. Rather, their very satisfied customers are out there selling on the salespeople's behalf, and these salespeople's jobs now consist of managing their customers as their own personal sales forces.

Any highly successful salesperson will tell you that the sale really begins *after* the sale. It's what you do for the customer after he says yes that is responsible for generating repeat or referral business. The one thing that all highly successful salespeople have in common is that the vast majority of their sales are the result of repeat and referral business. And customers don't supply you with repeat and referral business out of habit or obligation. Rather, repeat and referral business is a customer's way of saying "thank you" for a job well done. Repeat business and referrals are things that you have to earn.

## MAINTAINING THE AGREEMENT

Maintaining the agreement is probably the most immediate of the three maintenance activities because it has a direct impact on the customer's level of commitment. This is critical because highly committed customers not only follow through on their immediate promises but they feel compelled to tell others about their experience with you as well. There are three aspects to maintaining an agreement, all of which require action on the part of you, the salesperson. Each of these three aspects is described in the pages that follow.

### Prevent Buyer's Remorse

"Buyer's remorse" is that feeling you experience after you have agreed to something and then realize that there is no longer any way you can gracefully back out. Preventing buyer's remorse is especially important when you're dealing with someone for the first time and they aren't totally convinced you're going to follow through as you have promised. Over time, as trust builds between you and a customer, buyer's remorse becomes much less of an issue.

All of us have experienced buyer's remorse at one time or another. It's human nature to second-guess yourself after you've concluded a transaction with someone whose motives you are not sure of. The worst case of buyer's remorse I ever experienced occurred a number of years ago when I was passing through Chicago's O'Hare Airport wearing my army uniform. My mind was on getting home and not on dodging members of a religious cult who frequent airports. As I came out of security, a person who later turned out to be a member of this cult said, "How's it going Captain Reck? I was in the same unit as you were in Vietnam!" (My name tag and my rank and Second Field Force insignia were part of my uniform.) We immediately started chatting about our personal experiences in Vietnam, which suckered me into thinking this guy was okay. He went on to tell me that since getting out of the army, he had been working for a charitable organization that did wonderful things for the youth of America. He then handed me a copy of a book, which he said was his gift to me, and asked if I would be willing to make a contribution to his organization. Since he seemed like such a nice person, I automatically pulled out my wallet and handed him a ten-dollar bill. About thirty seconds later, it occurred to me that I had just been taken advantage of by a very slick salesperson. Buyer's remorse began to settle in as I felt both foolish and embarrassed.

As I looked down at my ten-dollar book, it was like looking at a mirror with the word "sucker" written all over it. I felt like a complete idiot. In an attempt to rid myself of this awful feeling, I threw the book into the nearest trash can only to find out later that nearly everyone who gets stuck with one of these books does the same thing, because they don't want the rest of the world to know they have just been had. This cult knows this and they pick through the trash cans to retrieve these symbols of buyer's remorse and sell them again. So I was taken advantage of twice by this group.

On the brighter side, however, that was the last time any such group took advantage of me. Because of that one experience, my guard is up anytime I walk through an airport or any other public place. Furthermore, I have taken it upon myself many times to intervene whenever I see a cult member trying to take advantage of some unsuspecting person.

Before customers will give you any repeat business or

refer others to you, they have to feel good about you, about what they have just bought, and about themselves for buying. If a customer experiences buyer's remorse, he probably won't come back again and he certainly won't refer any of his trusted friends to you. This is precisely why automobile companies engage in national advertising campaigns where they feature beautiful people driving their cars. These commercials are designed to make people who have already bought their cars feel good about their decision, and thus motivate them to sell their friends on the idea of buying one.

Preventing buyer's remorse requires that, after the customer says yes, you reinforce the idea that the customer can trust you and that you will, in fact, follow through on your promises. In other words, do whatever is necessary to keep the customer from feeling stuck. Several years ago, I purchased a swimming pool from Shasta Pool Company in Mesa, Arizona. The price of the pool was about $15,000, which was a significant amount of money for me. Given that I had never bought a pool before, this transaction harbored the potential for buyer's remorse.

The pool company knew this, however, and took direct and deliberate action to prevent it. A representative from the company held my hand throughout every phase of the construction process. Then, after the pool was installed, a representative from Shasta came out and explained how to correctly operate all the equipment. A week later, another representative came out to re-explain everything. A month later, yet another representative came out to answer any questions I had, and that representative came out again three months later. I also received several letters in the mail during that first year suggesting that if I was experiencing any problems or if I had any questions to please call them.

Each visit I received reinforced the idea that I had bought from the right pool company. At no time during the transaction did I ever feel stuck. As a result, today a lot of my friends have Shasta pools. Shasta saw to it that I felt good about the pool I bought and about myself for having bought it. They did not take me for granted after I said yes.

## Hold up Your End of the Agreement

By holding up your end of the agreement, you are seeing to it that the expectations of the customer, regarding you and your product or service, are being met. As Theodore Levitt said in *The Marketing Imagination*, "The object is to fulfill the customer's expectations so as to earn his loyalty and thus his continued patronage, preferably at a level of satisfaction that will be reflected in above-average margins." Fulfilling customer expectations is incredibly important because, as Levitt goes on to say, "*Expectations* are what people buy, not things. They buy the expectations of the benefits promised by the vendor."

The key to meeting customer expectations rests with providing good service that not only takes care of the customer's business needs, but his personal or ego needs as well. Surprisingly, this is not very difficult to accomplish as people are simply not used to receiving good service. So if you do anything at all in this area, you'll stand out. If you meet a customer's expectations, you'll surprise him; if you exceed his expectations, you'll shock him. It's this feeling of being surprised or shocked that turns a passive customer into a zealous evangelist on your behalf.

A good friend of mine used to work for American Express. As she was returning from a business trip, she found herself seated on a plane next to a company president who was upset with the runaround he was getting from the people at American Express who were trying to resolve a problem with his account. He was planning to cancel his corporate card when he got back to his office. As my friend listened to this man talk about his problem, she concluded that he was not getting proper treatment. She then asked for his business card and said she'd personally look into his problem on the very next day. I'm sure this company president said to himself, "I've heard that one before." At any rate, I don't think he ever expected a phone call from a director of American Express before noon on the following day. The director apologized to him for what had happened and told him that the problem had been resolved—which it had been. Needless to say, the company president was shocked, not only at the promptness of the action, but also at the fact that a director took it upon himself to make the phone call. Notice how this action took care of this person's business needs as well as his ego needs. To this day, this man is very high on doing business with American Express.

Recently I had the pleasure of visiting several departments in one of the regional operating centers of American Express. I came away very impressed with the high regard that everybody I talked to seemed to have for the customer. As one department manager told me, "our mission is to keep the cardmember spoiled." This mission symbolizes the commitment on the part of American Express to continually search for new and better ways to meet or exceed the expectations of its customers.

Nothing will diminish commitment faster, on the part of the customer, than his expectations not being met. Several years ago, I was at the Las Vegas airport awaiting the departure of a flight to South Bend, Indiana. I was a frequent flyer with the airline and at the time preferred it over most others. To make a long story short, my flight was canceled and there were no other flights that could get me into South Bend that evening.

The agent for the airline apologized profusely and told us all not to fret. She said the airline would pick up the bill for putting us up the extra night and she assured us of a seat on the first flight out the next morning. The situation, however, was compounded by the fact that it was Saturday night and nearly all the hotel rooms in Las Vegas were booked. The only room available was in a "flea bag" hotel strategically located, on the outskirts of town, between a topless restaurant and a massage parlor. Even though I was not happy with the accommodations, I didn't blame the airline because they couldn't help that it was Saturday night.

When dinnertime arrived, I decided to pass on the topless restaurant and took a cab back to town, which cost me $5.00 each way. I had dinner at a moderately priced restaurant and the bill came to $19.95, including the tip.

The next morning I went back to the airport to turn in my receipts, expecting to get reimbursed for my out-of-pocket expenses without a hassle. Was I in for a shock—the agent said she would not pay the $10.00 in cab fares. She said it was company policy not to do so. She also said she would allow me only $10.00 of the $19.95 that my dinner cost. She then proceeded to interrogate me on the rest of my expenses.

At this point, I asked to see the manager as I was beginning to become angry. It wasn't the money, because we were talking about only $20.00. Rather, it was the treatment. As a frequent flyer, I expected to be treated with at least a modicum of dignity, especially given what I had just endured because of the airline. My expectations were nowhere near being met.

When the manager arrived, I assured him that I was not at all angry with him and that I realized his hands were tied by the ridiculous set of company policies he had to enforce. He asked me why I thought they were ridiculous. I answered that for the $20.00 these policies were going to deny me, they were also going to motivate me to bad-mouth the airline. Out of frustration this manager said, "What should we do when a flight cancels, give each passenger a blank check?" My answer was "Absolutely!" I went on, "The airline ought to take such good care of people who have to endure canceled flights that they can't wait for such an incident to occur again." I further pointed out that this was how a company could turn its customers into a sales force, but for a lousy $20.00 this airline was going to do just the opposite.

The manager must have seen the logic in my argument

because he proceeded to pay me the $20.00 and he also upgraded me to first class. Although these gestures were nice, the airline could have had a far better impact on me had these considerations been granted without a hassle. To this day, even though things have changed at this airline with regard to customer service, I still think of my hassle in Las Vegas.

## Provide Meaningful Expressions of Appreciation to Customers Who Go the Extra Mile for You

This is absolutely essential if you want to turn your customers into an active and enthusiastic sales force. Whenever one of your customers goes the extra mile on your behalf, make sure you go out of your way to express your gratitude. If one of your customers refers another customer to you, don't let that behavior go unnoticed. Make a big deal out of expressing your appreciation. The idea is to make that person feel so good for having gone that extra mile for you that he can't wait for a chance to do it again and he can't keep his mouth shut about how great you are.

It doesn't hurt if you shock your customers a bit with the manner in which you express your appreciation. This, too, is not very difficult as most people are not used to being appreciated very much. Not long ago, I had the chance to sit on a plane next to a banquet manager for a large resort in the Phoenix area. This gentleman asked what I did for a living and I told him that one of the things I did was speak at sales meetings. He then gave me his card and asked me to send him some information about myself, as he occasionally was asked by meeting planners if he knew of any good speakers for a sales or management meeting. I thanked this person for his interest and when I returned to my office, I had an information packet sent to him.

About three months later, I received a phone call from a meeting planner who had been referred to me by this banquet manager. It turned out that she needed a quality speaker for a sales meeting and was willing to pay a sizable fee. I agreed to speak at that meeting, and it turned out to be a rousing success, which made the banquet manager look good to the meeting planner. When the program concluded, I took some time to tell the banquet manager how appreciative I was that he had referred me to this client. He said, "It's all part of my job."

As I walked to the parking lot of the resort, it occurred to me that this guy had just stuck his neck out for me and had put a large chunk of money in my pocket. He probably had a number of opportunities during the course of a year to recommend speakers for meetings and probably knew of a number of different speakers. I asked myself, "Did my thanking this person in the customary manner with a handshake, motivate him to recommend me ahead of all the other quality speakers he knew, or was there something more that I needed to do?" In other words, did I give this person sufficient reason to evangelize on my behalf?

After giving the matter some thought, I concluded that my personal thank you, even followed up with a handwritten note, probably wasn't sufficient motivation for him to become an active salesperson on my behalf. So I walked back into the resort and spoke with one of the person's coworkers. I found out this banquet manager had a fondness for quality Scotch whiskey and he loved to eat out at restaurants. This gave me some ideas.

Several days later, I made an appointment to meet with the banquet manager. Upon meeting him, I again personally thanked him for having recommended me. I presented him with a quart of Chivas Regal as a token of my appreciation, which caught him completely by surprise. Then I handed him a $50 "Be My Guest" voucher from American Express, which would allow him to take someone to dinner at a restaurant of his choice. At this point the banquet manager had to sit down. He said that he was shocked, that no one had ever done something like that for him before, and that he was very appreciative of the gesture.

Please keep in mind that the amount of money involved was minimal compared to his salary and the fee that was involved. What is important is that I demonstrated to this person that I sincerely appreciated his having gone the extra mile on my behalf. Since then, this banquet manager has become one of my best salespeople and has recommended me to numerous other meetings and conferences. Each time he does so, I let him know, in a meaningful way, that his extra efforts on my behalf were sincerely appreciated.

Another example of taking care of customers who go the extra mile involves the department store chain Nordstrom. Nordstrom has long been known for the way it takes care of its customers. I live in Phoenix, Arizona, where there is no Nordstrom. The closest stores are located in San Diego or Los Angeles, some 300 miles away or one hour by air. So how do you get people from Phoenix to come to San Diego to shop at Nordstrom? The answer is that you take incredibly good care of the people who do and they will spread the word.

Each June and November, in conjunction with their major sales, Nordstrom schedules its "Sky Trip" from Phoenix. They fly in 250 shoppers on Friday afternoon for an all-day Saturday and Sunday shopping trip. Each shopper pays $175 to be part of this group.

Why would anyone pay $175 to fly to San Diego and spend the majority of their time shopping at a store that isn't known for its low prices? Let me tell you what you get for that $175 price tag. First, the trip includes your round trip-air fare, deluxe accommodations at the Doubletree Hotel, shuttle service to and from the airport, and a champagne welcome when you arrive. But that is not all. On Saturday morning, a shuttle takes you to the store, where you are issued a pin that identifies you as a "Sky Trip" participant. This pin entitles the wearer to some very preferential treatment. You receive faster service because certain employees have been assigned to stand in the cash register line for you so you can continue to shop uninterrupted. These same employees have also been assigned to maintain a fitting room for you while you shop. They follow you around and take the things you are interested in trying on to the fitting room while you continue to browse. Once you have decided it's time to actually try on some of these articles of clothing, these helpers are at your beck and call to search the store over for that special blouse or accessory that will make a certain outfit complete.

There is still more. A special room in the store has been set aside for these shoppers from Phoenix where they can get a continental breakfast in the morning and coffee, tea, and so on throughout the day, as well as a box lunch. These shoppers are encouraged to use the room if they need to take an occasional break. They can also leave their paid-for packages in this room, as people are assigned to make sure this room is secure. Also, on Sunday morning the store is open exclusively to the "Fly and Shop" customers. These shoppers are pampered to death by Nordstrom's employees and they thoroughly love every second of it.

So what's the payoff to Nordstrom for all this pampering? Most of the customers do buy a fair amount of merchandise. More important, however, these people get on their return flights to Phoenix very excited about their experience. So excited, that many of them plan for their next "Sky Trip" six months down the road. Even more important, however, for the next six weeks, these people never stop talking about their wonderful experience at Nordstrom—and Phoenicians go to San Diego a lot. It used to be there were three highlights to one of these excursions: the ocean, the San Diego Zoo, and Sea World. Today, there's a fourth: Nordstrom.

What this all boils down to is that you have to remember to take care of the people who are taking care of you. As long as you continue to meaningfully reinforce your customers' going the extra mile on your behalf, they'll continue to do so. The minute you take your customers for granted and ignore their extra efforts, you'll find yourself back to having to do everything by yourself.

## MAINTAINING THE RELATIONSHIP

If you want to keep your customers out there hustling on your behalf, you must see to it that the relationship between you and each one of them is properly maintained. The types of activities required to maintain these relationships are so simple and obvious that they are often overlooked and their importance is often ignored. Highly successful salespeople engage in these activities with a sense of passion and purpose because they are very much aware of the payoff.

In *The Marketing Imagination*, Theodore Levitt addressed the importance of maintaining the buyer-seller relationship when he wrote, "The sale merely consummates the courtship. Then the marriage begins. How good the marriage is depends on how well the relationship is managed by the seller. That determines whether there will be continued or expanded business or troubles and divorce, and whether costs or profits increase." Like a marriage, a buyer-seller relationship requires that the two parties spend some time visiting and communicating with each other at the personal level. Although there is nothing wrong with exchanging business-related information when you get together with a customer, it is very important to the maintenance of your relationship that these information exchanges are supplemented by some socializing. You must engage in conversation or activity that is fun and you must show a personal interest in him. Just as trust is created through personal feelings, it has to be maintained at the personal level.

Continue to spend some time visiting with your customers when you're not trying to sell them anything. Taking a customer to lunch, dropping by just to say hello, and asking how things are going are the ways to maintain relationships. If you can't visit each of your customers as often as you would like, then drop them a personal note or give them a phone call between visits to let them know you're still thinking of them. As Walter D. Moody wrote so eloquently in his book, *Men Who Sell Things*, published back in 1907, "You cannot personally shake hands and jolly up your customers every few days; so the next best thing is to write them personal letters, just as you would talk to them if you were to meet them on the street or in their places of business. Naturally, the more personal talks you can have with your customers, the better; but in-between trips write them a heart-to-heart letter now and then, just to make them feel you are keeping them in mind."

A recent consulting experience with a major manufacturer of science equipment also drove home the importance of salespeople maintaining relationships with customers. This particular company had one major competitor with whom they went head-to-head on nearly every one of their products. The products of these two competitors looked the same and worked the same, so they were basically interchangeable. The only differences were the color of the lettering on the products and the logo. The problem this particular company was asking me to solve was why they had lost 25 percent of their market share during the past two years.

The first question I asked was whether or not their quality had slipped relative to their competitors. The answer I got was "Not at all!" The next question I asked was whether or not their level of customer service had fallen off. Again, the answer was an emphatic "no." I went on to ask a series of additional questions and received similar answers. Finally, I asked if they had experienced any turnover in their field sales force. As it turned out, this company had forty field salespeople who covered all of North America and they had lost nine of these people during the past two years due to retirement.

Hearing that they had lost nearly 25 percent of their sales force during the same two years that they had lost 25 percent of their market share, I became curious. The rest of the conversation went as follows:

"How long had these people been in the field representing your company before they retired?" I asked.

The vice-president of sales answered, "Between twenty-five and thirty years."

"Who did you replace these people with?" I asked.

"New college hires," answered one of the regional managers.

"What are the career aspirations of these new college hires?"

The vice-president of sales was beginning to sense the real cause of the problem when he answered, "They want to gut it out in the field for a year and a half to two years, then get into corporate marketing."

"There's the problem," I said. "Those people who had been in the field for twenty-five to thirty years had built very solid relationships with their customers. As a result, their customers were very loyal to them. Since both your and your competition's products are virtually the same, those customers bought from the salesperson who they had the strongest relationship with, which just happened to be your salesperson.

"When those salespeople retired, their relationships did not automatically carry over to their replacements. Because their replacements had no interest in staying in the field, they saw no reason to invest energy into building their own relationships with their customers. As a result, customers shifted their loyalty to the competitor's salespeople, each of whom had been working on their own customer relationships for quite some time."

I then looked at the vice-president of sales and said, "You've been thinking all along that your customers were buying your products because these products had your brand name on them. The reality, however, is that years ago they bought these respective salespeople who, coincidentally, just happened to be carrying your product line!"

What had happened over the years was that top management had gotten carried away with managing products and had totally forgotten about managing customers. In just two years, this misplaced emphasis had cost them 25 percent of their market share! The vice-president of sales was especially upset because he knew these customers would be very difficult to win back. He had now come to realize that customer loyalty is not just a matter of advertising and promotion, it's a matter of managing customer relationships.

Joe Girard, the world's greatest new car salesperson, provides us with some classic examples on how to maintain relationships. Joe saw to it that his customers never forgot him once they bought a car from him. Joe's customers were hardly out of the door before a thank-you note had been made up for them. They received a letter once a month thereafter. (His mailing list contained more than 13,000 names.) Each letter carried a simple message appropriate to the month such as "Happy New Year" or "Happy Valentine's Day," and it was signed: "Joe Girard, Merollis Chevrolet." These letters contained absolutely no sales pitch, and they communicated the fact that Joe hadn't forgotten about them. Finally, whenever a customer came in to get his car repaired or serviced, Joe made sure he used this opportunity to personally visit with the customer and reinforce the fact that he still genuinely cared about him as a human being. If the customer was experiencing a problem, Joe would even go to bat for him to make sure he was treated fairly. Joe truly cared about each customer and each one of them knew it. This is why he sold more cars, for eleven consecutive years, than any other human being.

Some relatives of mine, Dick and Lucille, own and manage a hardware store in a small town in Michigan. The hardware store they own is part of a chain of hardware stores that specializes in serving small communities. When Dick and Lucille moved to this community twenty years ago, they became part of it. They lived there, their kids went to school there, and they went to church there. When they opened their store, as people came in, they welcomed them warmly, eventually got to know them, and each time they came back, treated them as friends. Dick and Lucille *never* tried to sell them anything. As a result of this honest, sincere, and friendly treatment, these customers came back time and again, and Dick and Lucille's business blossomed.

About eight years ago, a competing hardware store chain built a new and much larger hardware store about a half-mile south of town by the freeway. Needless to say, Dick and Lucille were very concerned that they would lose many of their customers to this new and much larger store.

As it turned out, many of their regular customers did go to that new store—but all they did was look. Yes, the store was larger and much more modern than Dick and Lucille's store and the prices on some items were a little lower. But there was no warm and friendly greeting as these customers walked into this new store. There was no old friend to chew the fat with while he was custom-cutting a piece of plastic pipe for you. And there was no resident expert whom you could ask what the fish were biting on that week. In other words, this new store may have had any piece of hardware or appliance you could possibly want, but it didn't have Dick and Lucille.

None of Dick and Lucille's regular customers switched their allegiance to this new store and several years later it closed. On the other hand, Dick and Lucille's business is better than ever. What killed this new store is that the people who ran it assumed that people went to a hardware store to buy hardware, and that they would go where they could get the best possible deal, even if it were a matter of only a few cents in price. At Dick and Lucille's store, however, customers came in to visit with Dick and Lucille; and while they were there, they picked up any hardware items they happened to need. What this proves is that if you treat your customers fairly and maintain your personal relationships with them, you literally lock out the competition.

## MAINTAINING THE PLAN

Turning a customer into an active salesperson on your behalf implies a long-term mutual commitment. As part of
this commitment, the customer expects that the product or
service you are selling will change over time in order to
meet any changes in his needs. This responsibility should
not be taken lightly, because the minute your customers
see your product or service as no longer satisfying their
current needs, they are likely to take their business
elsewhere—regardless of all that you have done for them in
the past! As W. Edwards Demming, the manufacturing
quality guru, put it in one of his speeches, "Profit and
growth come from the loyal customer who can boast about
your product or service. He requires no advertising or other
persuasion, is willing to wait in line, and brings a friend
along with him. It is therefore the obligation of the pro-
ducer to foresee the needs of his customer and to produce
for him a new design, new product, new service. We must
constantly strive to stay ahead of the needs of the customer."

The key to staying ahead of customer needs is simply
*listening.* If you listen long enough and hard enough, the
customer will tell you exactly what it's going to take to
maintain his loyalty. As simple as this sounds, however,
most of us don't listen very well, especially to our customers. We tend to be preoccupied with our own problems
and needs rather than those of our customers. And, as I've
said, listening to our customers is sometimes perceived as
an unpleasant task because the only time they seem to
want to tell us anything is when they want to complain
about something.

In reality, however, listening to customer complaints
should be viewed as a positive experience for a number of
reasons. First of all, customer complaints are a sign of a

healthy relationship. As Theodore Levitt said in *The Marketing Imagination*, "One of the surest signs of a bad or declining relationship is the absence of complaints from the customer. The customer is either not being candid or not being contacted. Probably both. Communication is impaired. The absence of candor reflects the decline of trust, the deterioration of the relationship."

Secondly, the vast majority of new product and service ideas come from customer complaints about current products or services. This is why highly successful companies have intentional, proactive programs to solicit complaints from customers. These companies cherish customer complaints and regard them as unparalleled opportunities to become even better at what they are already very good at. Thus, an important aspect of your job as a salesperson ought to be regularly asking your customers questions like: "How am I doing?" "What could I be doing better?" "Are there any areas where I am falling short or not keeping up?" "Is the current product or service I am offering you going to meet your future needs?"

Taking the time to actively listen to the answers to questions like these will give you the information you need to keep up with your customers' changing needs. But you have to be willing to spend the time, which is an activity that isn't always encouraged by those around you. *In Search of Excellence* by Tom Peters and Robert Waterman makes this point very well. Peters and Waterman tell of a sales executive who was reflecting on his first job. He said, "I spent forever getting to know a small handful of customers really well. It paid off handsomely. I came in at 195 percent of quota, tops in my division. A fellow at corporate called me and said, 'Good job, to be sure, but you averaged only 1.2 sales calls a day and the company averages 4.6. Just think of what you could sell if you could get your average up to par!' You can guess my response after I came down off the ceiling; I said, 'Just think what the rest could sell if they could get their average *down* to 1.2.'"

The reason this salesperson was so successful was that

he was taking the time to listen to his customers and then using this information to make sure his product or service was tailored to satisfy each customer's current needs. He was able to work smarter instead of harder, which paid off handsomely for him. As Tom Peters said during a speech several years ago, "If you listen to what your customers have to say and then do something about it, the bottom line is, you'll get filthy rich!"

For example, the Marriott hotel chain has been one of the more successful hotel chains over the years. One of the primary reasons for its success is that it puts customer complaint forms *everywhere*, even by the pay phones! Legend has it that up until just a few years before his death, J. W. Marriott, Sr., the founder of the company, read many of these complaint forms and answered them personally. He also immediately saw to it that something was done to alleviate the cause of the complaint. Doing this helped Marriott, as chief executive of his company, stay in touch with his customers and their changing needs over time. In addition, during their next stay at a Marriott hotel, when these customers saw that the problem they complained about had been taken care of, they were assured that Marriott took their patronage seriously.

So: Make it easy for your customers to complain. Actively solicit their inputs about you and your product or service. Then act on these inputs. If you do this and do it well, you'll not only stay ahead of your competition, *you won't have any competition.*

# CHAPTER EIGHT

# Using the PRAM Model as a Diagnostic Tool

ONE OF THE important advantages of the PRAM Model is that it is incredibly useful as a diagnostic and problem-solving tool. I haven't found a human interaction problem yet where I couldn't pinpoint the cause of the problem within one of the four steps of the PRAM Model. A problem can be a planning problem, a relationship problem, an agreement problem, or a maintenance problem, and once you locate its cause, you can then prescribe a course of action to resolve the problem.

I have a friend who is a telemarketer and schedules speaking engagements for me. One day she called to ask me tentatively to hold a date for a program in Tucson. After we had finished our business, I decided it was time to do a little relationship maintenance with her. So I asked her how it was going. She told me things had been going fine until that afternoon when the school principal called to tell her they were sending her teenage son home because of a behavioral problem. She went on to say that the problem had been brewing for quite a while and she was very frustrated because her son was capable of becoming a straight-A student, but he refused to apply himself.

Although it was probably none of my business, I asked her how she planned to deal with the situation. She told me she planned to sit down at the kitchen table that evening with her husband and her son and they were going to work out a solution to the problem once and for all. Then she asked me what I thought. As she had read *The Win-Win Negotiator* and attended one of my seminars, she was very familiar with the PRAM Model, so I used it in structuring my response. I pointed out that although the method by which she planned to resolve the problem seemed very logical to her, in reality she was trying to throw an agreement formation (Step Three) solution at a relationship (Step Two) problem. I went on to tell her that although I didn't want to be the one to deliver the bad news, it was my assessment that her son didn't trust her or her husband.

At first this woman became rather defensive at the notion that her son didn't trust her and pointed out that the three members of her family had lived together for fourteen years. How could they not trust each other? I asked if she ever visited her son in his room. She responded that she did so at least a half-dozen times a week. I asked if most of the visits were pleasant and relaxed, or confrontational in nature: Did she ask him things like, How come your room is such a mess? and, You promised you'd mow the lawn yesterday, why isn't it done? and, When are you going to get your act together at school?

She quickly admitted that almost all her visits to her son's room were confrontational in nature. I pointed out that if this were the case, her son didn't even like it when she entered his room because he knew it would be an unpleasant experience. She asked me what she should do. My response was that until the trust level was raised and her son felt good and comfortable with her and her husband, there would be no progress with his behavior at school. So I recommended that she and her husband work on the trust problem first. I suggested she and her husband each spend fifteen minutes alone with their son every night for the following two weeks, talking about whatever their son wanted to talk about, without hassling him about anything. I asked them not to bring up the school problem until after these two weeks were over and to avoid any other types of confrontations with him during that period. In addition, I also asked them to go out of their way on a couple of occasions to make their son feel special.

Ten days later, I received a phone call from this woman to confirm my speaking date in Tucson. When we had finished talking business, I asked her how the family situation was going. She told me that both she and her husband had done exactly what I had recommended. She did admit, however, it had taken her a few evenings to get used to going into her son's room and not hassling him. They also had gone out of their way to make him feel special by taking him to an electronics show that he was very interested in. She went on to say that as a result of all this, the problem at school had taken care of itself. It was never even brought up. She also told me that on the previous day, her son had come home from school and said to her, "Guess what happened in school today, Mom?" She said that he hadn't said anything like that since the first grade!

Amazing results can be achieved in solving problems when you apply an appropriate solution to the true problem. Results like those described above can become commonplace in your dealings with other people, especially your customers. The key to realizing such results is to correctly diagnose the cause of the problem *before* you attempt to apply a solution. And it's the PRAM Model that holds the key to an accurate diagnosis.

In the sections that follow, some of the more common problems that salespeople encounter will be presented. The PRAM Model will then be applied as a diagnostic tool in order to pinpoint the actual cause of each of these problems. Once the cause of the problem has been determined, possible solutions will be discussed.

## COLD CALLS

Cold calls are first-time calls on new prospects. Salespeople by and large do not like making cold calls. In fact, many of them absolutely hate it. The reason is that cold calls have such a high failure or rejection rate associated with them. As Tom Peters said in *Thriving on Chaos*, "Anyone who's been a salesperson for even a day agrees that there's no lousier way to live than depending on cold calls."

Cold calls have such a high failure rate because of the philosophy underlying the traditional approach to selling; that is, "The name of the game is to *get the order.*" Adherence to this philosophy has led to a belief that the success of a sales call is judged as based upon whether the salesperson got the order. For this reason, salespeople operating under the traditional approach to selling feel duty bound to push for the order whenever they make a sales call, including cold calls.

The PRAM Model provides us with insight as to why this approach results in such a high failure rate. By pushing for the order on the first meeting, a salesperson is trying to get to yes without having successfully avoided no. As I have stated, people prefer to say yes to people they like and trust. The problem with cold calls is that no relationship, and hence no trust, exists between the salesperson and the customer. By pushing for the order in the absence of such trust, the salesperson is telling the customer that he is more interested in the customer's money than he is in the customer's welfare. Because no one likes to do business with a hustler, the customer generally says no, which the salesperson interprets as rejection or failure.

The thing to keep in mind if you want to become a highly successful salesperson is that you are after the business and not merely the order. Your objective is to eventually turn a new prospect into a long-term source of repeat and referral business. Doing this requires that you first build a relationship of trust between you and the customer *before* you try to sell him anything. Thus, on a first-time call, your goal should not be to sell the customer anything, but rather to initiate a relationship. Subsequent visits should be used as opportunities to cultivate the relationship and demonstrate that you are genuinely interested in the customer and his or her welfare. As Joe Gandolfo put it in his book, *How to Make Big Money Selling*, "Every super-successful salesperson that I've ever met comes across as a thoughtful, loving, caring individual who knows inner peace. It's a tough image to fake! . . . You've got to project sincerity and put the customer's interests first. Study successful salespeople. Their customers *always* come first. With this approach, the money automatically comes. But when the money is put first, success is usually a long way down the road."

A number of my clients have rewritten the job descriptions of their salespeople. As part of these new job descriptions, cold calling, with its unpleasant rejection rate, has been replaced with *relationship calling*: Salespeople in these organizations are expected to spend a certain percentage of their time initiating and cultivating relationships with new prospects, without the pressure of having to make an immediate sale. The reward structure in these organizations has also been expanded—it's no longer based totally on the amount of sales for a given period but now includes incentives for relationship-building activities and for sales obtained as a result of repeat and referral business. These revised job descriptions and expanded reward systems are consistent with what Tom Peters prescribed in *Thriving on Chaos*: "Sales commissions and/or salaries ought to be skewed substantially toward incentives for repeat and add-on business. . . . Repeat and add-on business usually results from a host of small but, in total, time-consuming touches . . . our incentives should say unequivocally, 'Spend the time!' "

## OBJECTIONS

We all have dealt with customers who need and can afford the products or services that we are selling but who balk when asked to say yes. These customers do so by drawing on an arsenal of excuses that allow them to avoid saying yes without having to directly say no. They may say that they need to consult their spouse or their attorney or that they'd like more time to shop around. Such excuses are often referred to as *objections.*

The PRAM Model provides us with insight as to why a customer objects. If you have done your planning from a Win-Win perspective, and if you've developed a relationship with the customer that is based on mutual trust, he or she is not going to throw out obstacles that get in the way of saying yes. At this point, assuming he or she needs your product or service and can afford it, then he or she wants to do business with you and will be willing to work out the details for everybody's benefit. As Tony Alessandra said in a speech at a national conference of the American Society for Training and Development, "If a customer doesn't want to do business with you, the details will always get in the way. If he does want to do business with you, the details will rarely get in the way."

In other words, when a customer objects, he is communicating that, for one reason or another, he doesn't trust you but he doesn't want to tell you to your face. When this occurs, it's time for you to go back to Step Two of the PRAM Model and work on the relationship. Try to find out what is causing the trust problem. It could be that you are pushing too hard for the sale and the customer is beginning to wonder if you're more concerned about getting his money than you are about him. Maybe you're trying to get the customer to say yes before he feels comfortable enough with you to do so. Or, maybe you haven't convinced the customer that you truly understand and appreciate his problem. In other words, the customer is objecting to *you*, not your product or service.

This is not the time for you to get argumentative or defensive. Don't try to show the customer why his objections are invalid. If you do, you run the risk of winning an argument and losing a customer. Rather, this is the time for you to back off, affirm or reaffirm to the customer that you genuinely care about him and his welfare, and get away from trying to sell him. The customer will buy when he's ready and feels comfortable, and not before.

## IRATE CUSTOMERS

Most salespeople would agree that dealing with an irate customer is, at best, an unpleasant experience. Customers who are upset can be very animated, vocal, and emotional. For this reason, many salespeople would rather avoid confrontations with an irate customer, choosing instead to write him off as a lost cause. Highly successful salespeople, on the other hand, have found that once you understand the motivation behind the customer's irate behavior, it's not at all unpleasant to deal with it. In fact, highly successful salespeople view dealing with an irate customer as a golden opportunity to sell this person for life and to turn him into an active evangelist on the salesperson's behalf.

Once again, the PRAM Model provides us with insight. When a customer becomes upset, it's generally because his expectations of what was to happen after he reached his agreement with you were not met. Irate behavior on the part of a customer is therefore a *maintenance* issue. The key in dealing with irate customers is for you not to take it personally. Try to keep in mind that you would probably react in a similar manner if you were in his shoes.

More importantly, however, try to keep in mind that these unmet expectations also represent a blow to the customer's ego. He bought a product or service from you because he expected you would deliver what you had promised and he now thinks you let him down. What you need to do to rectify the situation is to restore his ego by showing that you still really care about him. You can do this by taking swift and decisive action to right the situation to the total satisfaction of the customer.

What's especially effective is to shock the irate customer a bit with how well you respond. True, it might cost you a few extra dollars, but it will buy you tons of loyalty and it will give these customers a reason to spread the word on your behalf. For example, several years ago, the Smiths, who are friends of mine, decided to take a trip to Amsterdam on People Express Airlines. They chose People Express because the fare was only $79 each way. It's too bad that People Express is no longer in business, because the way in which they handled the situation that I'm about to describe was nothing short of superb.

Every aspect of the trip came off without a hitch until it was time to make the return trip from Amsterdam to Newark Airport. The flight was several hours late, and this meant the connecting time for the couple who lived in Hartford would be very, very short. When the flight arrived in Newark, everyone was very tired and a bit on edge. As the couple headed for Hartford stepped off the plane, they asked an airport employee (not a People Express employee) for directions to the Hartford flight. As fate would have it, the airport employee sent them in the wrong direction and they missed their connecting flight. Needless to say, they no longer thought very kindly of People Express, even if the fare was only $79.

As they were walking back toward the gate from which the connecting flight had already taken off, they were met by a well-groomed representative of People Express who was accompanied by a skycap. As she approached the couple, the airline representative said, "Obviously you are Mr. and Mrs. Smith." The Smiths nodded their heads, somewhat shocked that this representative not only knew their name but came looking for them as well. The representative apologized for the incident and asked them to give their bags to the skycap and come with her to where they could look at their options in more comfortable surroundings.

The representative took the couple to a comfortable lounge area. She then pointed out that People Express's next flight to Hartford wasn't for four more hours and asked the couple if they would mind driving. Anxious to get home, the couple agreed that driving was a better option than waiting at the airport for four hours. The airline representative said, "Very well. The skycap has your bags and he will take them to a cab that is out front waiting for you. The skycap has already been tipped and the cab driver has been paid and tipped, courtesy of People Express. The cab will take you to a rental car agency where a car is being prepared for you so that you can be on your way home without further delay. The rental car fee is also being paid for by People Express. On behalf of People Express, I am very sorry you had to suffer this inconvenience. I hope it never happens again and here are two free round-trip tickets good to anywhere People Express flies to compensate you for the inconvenience."

You can imagine the look on the couple's faces when the airline representative handed them the two free tickets. They were both shocked and impressed by the way People Express took a negative situation and turned it into a positive one. Again, it's too bad that People Express is out of business, because I have shared that incident with thousands of people over the last several years, all because I was so impressed with the classy way this and similar situations were handled. I had never flown People Express, yet this airline was able to turn me into one of its most enthusiastic salespeople.

Setting a situation right to the satisfaction of a disappointed customer may involve a little extra effort on your part and may even cost you a few extra dollars. But it certainly pays off. As Tom Peters wrote in *Thriving on Chaos*, "A well-handled problem usually breeds more loyalty than you had before the negative incident." Very often, properly taking care of disappointed customers is what will set you apart from the masses.

## WHY AREN'T THERE MORE MILLIONAIRES?

Several years ago, when I was conducting a seminar in Omaha, one of the participants stood up and asked, "If the PRAM Model is so simple and works so well, how come there aren't more millionaires?" I must admit the question caught me by surprise, so I immediately called for a break so that I could think about the answer. As I mulled this question around in my mind, it began to occur to me that the reason there aren't more millionaires, or highly successful people in any endeavor for that matter, is that most people don't recognize the importance that relationships play in being successful in any profession. As such, these people don't devote any effort toward developing these necessary relationships because they don't see the need. Without these relationships, however, they are unable to enlist the active support of other people on their behalf and so are destined to go through life trying to do everything by themselves. As I stated very early in this book, the one common thread that links all highly successful people together is that they have an army of friends standing in line just waiting for the chance to do them a favor.

Not long ago, I gave a speech to a group of people in Atlanta and as I talked about this very issue, I noticed a woman in the audience who was literally bouncing up and down in her chair with enthusiasm. When my speech was over, she came up to me, shook my hand and said, "Please forgive me for being so excited, but my father is a self-made millionaire and there isn't a day that goes by when he doesn't get at least one phone call from someone asking if there is anything they can do for him." She went on to say, "I thought you would want to know that your formula works!"

On my return trip from Atlanta to Phoenix I had to change planes in Dallas. As I took my seat, I recognized the person sitting next to me. His name was Bill King and he was the owner of a very successful chain of brake repair shops known as Bill King's Brake-O. I had seen him many times in his television commercials.

As the two of us got to know each other, Bill King began to share with me his philosophy on success. At one point, he leaned back and said, "Ross, let me tell you from personal experience that the road to becoming a millionaire is so simple that it boggles most people's minds."

I thought to myself, "Mr. King, you keep talking, because I am taking notes!"

He went on, "If you develop a sense of trust with your employees [relationships] and take good care of them [maintenance], your employees will take good care of you. Furthermore, if you develop a sense of trust with your customers [relationships] and take good care of them [maintenance], your customers will take good care of you." He then said, "If you want to make a million dollars a year, you need a million friends each turning a dollar a year for you. Or, you need a half-million friends each turning you two dollars per year and so forth. If you work this process long enough, you'll eventually develop enough friends who each generate the right amount of revenue on your behalf. Once that happens," he concluded, "being a millionaire is a piece of cake."

I remember saying, "No wonder wealthy people don't seem to work so hard!"

Bill King laughed at my remark because he had just spent several days participating in a golf tournament. He did say, however, that developing all these necessary relationships doesn't happen overnight. It takes time, and it's work. On the other hand, it has a virtually guaranteed payoff. Take care of the people who stand between you and success or failure and they will take care of you.

# CHAPTER NINE

# Becoming a Highly Successful Salesperson

THERE ARE THREE very important concepts you must apply each and every time you put the PRAM Model to use. These are *balance, integrity,* and *patience.* Applying these concepts to the PRAM Model will enable you to turn your customers into a sales force. If you ignore these concepts, you can expect only mediocre results at best.

## BALANCE

As you look at the PRAM Model, one of the things you will notice is that each of the four steps is equal in size. This means that each of the four steps is of equal importance. This does not mean that each of the four steps will take the same amount of time, but it does mean that you can't afford to ignore or skip any of these steps if you expect to achieve a high level of success. Look at the PRAM Model as if it were a baseball diamond. If you want to make a score, two things are essential. First, you must touch all four bases, and second, *you must touch them in the correct order.*

Probably the most common business problem today is going from Step One (Planning) directly to Step Three (Agreement Formation) without going through Step Two (Relationship Development). This is especially true in selling and is one of the primary reasons there aren't more highly successful salespeople. In other words, all too often salespeople try to sell their product or service before they successfully sell themselves.

Recently, I gave a talk to the scouting staff of the Chicago Cubs baseball team. When I had concluded my talk, I asked these people to share some of the problems they encountered in trying to sign high school recruits. These scouts told me that the biggest problem they faced was the increased competition they were getting from colleges and universities trying to recruit the same players. They made it very clear that they did not want to lure away kids who would benefit from attending a college or university. They were concerned with those who were not ready for college and who would be better off going directly from high school to a minor league baseball team.

They did admit they had relatively little problem signing a first-, second-, or third-round draft choice because they could pay these people anywhere from $60,000 to $150,000 per year. The problem was with the lower-round draft choices. For example, a twelfth-round draft choice received only $700 per month and $12 per day for meal money. On the other hand, a college scholarship could be worth as much as $15,000 per year, depending on the institution, and colleges and universities paid $15 per day for meal money.

The scouts went on and on about how more money would solve the problem. Finally, I suggested that they might be attempting to throw a Step Three (Agreement Formation) solution at a Step Two (Relationship Development) problem. I said it looked to me like the colleges and universities weren't winning the recruiting war against them with more money. Rather, they were doing a better job of building relationships with the players. I pointed out that these college coaches probably came across as a big brother or father figure, while the players on these college teams probably came across as a great bunch of guys to hang around with. If this were the case, making more money available for minor league salaries was not going to solve their problem.

As I finished my statement, three senior scouts stood up and enthusiastically confirmed my assessment. They went on to say that in years past they had made it a point to build relationships with every young man they were even remotely interested in because it was an open market and a high school graduate could sign with any team. Under such circumstances, it was very important to develop relationships—a high school recruit generally signed with the team whose scouting staff he felt most comfortable with. Recently, however, high school recruiting had become subject to a draft and the player could only sign with the team that drafted him. Most scouting personnel no longer see a need to develop relationships with all the players that they might be interested in because there is only a one-in-twenty-six chance that they will be able to draft any one of them. Relationship building was no longer a high priority for most scouts.

One of these senior scouts, however, said that he had continued his relationship-building activities in spite of the draft. As a result, he rarely loses a player that he recruits to a college or university. He then went on to explain his method of building relationships with high school baseball players. He holds baseball clinics on Saturdays throughout his territory during the warm-weather months. He enlists the support of some former major league ball players and then he invites approximately thirty to forty boys to participate in each clinic. At these clinics, this scout provides instruction on some of the finer points of hitting and playing defense. These players are then given a chance to try out these new ideas in a game among themselves.

In addition to assessing each boy's potential, the goal of this scout in putting on these clinics is to make sure that he or one of his assistants interacts with each boy individually in a very positive way. For example, he told of a boy who, while batting, popped the ball straight up in the air for an out. At this point the scout halted the game and told the boy that the reason he popped the ball up was because he dipped his shoulder when he swung at the ball. He asked this boy to come back and take a few more swings while concentrating on keeping his shoulders square. After a couple of pitches, this boy was hitting the ball squarely and was very impressed that this man had taken the time to correct the problem. The scout then went over to the sideline where a pitcher was warming up. He asked the pitcher if he would like to learn how to throw a split-fingered fast ball. The boy nodded yes and the scout proceeded to show him the finer points of how to throw the pitch. This boy, too, was very impressed that a scout for a major league team would take the time to give him some special attention. Because of all this warm, positive attention, at the end of the clinic, the enthusiastic consensus among the boys was "We sure hope the Cubs draft us, because we want to play baseball for the Cubs!"

This scout did not view his job as ending once he got a recruit to say yes to the Cubs. He went on to point out that there was still more a scout could do to make his job easier. He kept very close track of all the players in his territory who had been drafted and signed and he periodically followed up to make sure that things were going well and that the Cubs were honoring all the promises he had made to them. By effectively performing this maintenance activity, he was able to turn these former recruits into a sales force on his behalf. The word got back to the high schools in his territory that the Cubs were a good team to play for and that he was a good person to deal with. This made his future recruiting efforts even easier.

## INTEGRITY

In order for the PRAM Model to deliver the results that I have promised, it has to be applied with genuine integrity. Trying to use the PRAM Model to manipulate people will eventually expose you as a fraud and I guarantee that no one will be standing in line to help you become highly successful.

During my last year as a professor of management at Arizona State University, the faculty development office undertook a project to assist faculty members to become better teachers. The project involved, first, identifying the seventy-five best teachers on the ASU campus. Next, a representative of the faculty development office was to administer a questionnaire to the students in each of these seventy-five teachers' classes. The instructions asked the students to evaluate their professor on a number of items such as level of preparation, enthusiasm for the subject, and so forth.

After the questionnaires had been administered, they were collected and the data run through a computer in order to find out at which of the items each professor was highly successful. Once this was known, a representative from the faculty development office interviewed each faculty member in an attempt to find out what he or she did that made him or her so successful. The idea was to put the results in the form of a handbook that would serve as a guide to help less-effective teachers improve themselves.

I was fortunate enough to be included among the seventy-five best teachers at ASU. Six weeks after the questionnaires were administered, a person from the faculty development office showed up at my office to go over the results with me. This turned out to be a very pleasant experience for me as she pointed out that I had scored very well. What she said next, however, really caught my attention because it revealed to me the ultimate secret to being successful at any people-oriented profession or activity.

She said there was one item that stood out from all the rest. This was that my students had the idea that I genuinely cared about them. As she told me this, she looked at me and said, "Now I want to know how you pulled that off!"

Since the question caught me off guard, I really didn't have an answer. I did, however, inform her of some of the things I did for my students such as helping those who were interested become straight-A students, helping them find high-paying jobs after they graduated, and treating them like friends instead of second-class citizens. After she thought for a moment, she looked up and said, "What you're telling me is you really do care and it shows." I must admit, this comment hit me like a ton of bricks because it had never occurred to me before. Yes, I did care, but caring was something I did as a matter of course with everyone. I had been taught to do so by my parents and I didn't know any other way to operate.

Reflecting back on my ten years as a professor at ASU, I remember receiving a lot of good-natured kidding from some of my colleagues. Some of them told me I spent far too much time with my students. Others told me that my salary level didn't warrant my giving those students the level of service that I did. I would acknowledge their comments and point out that it was the one aspect of my job that I really enjoyed. Interestingly enough, when I resigned my position and went into business for myself, my income immediately tripled, and 80 percent of my business during the first two years I was out on my own came from my ex-students. Until recently, I had never associated the idea of caring about people as having any sort of payoff, but it really does. What goes around definitely does come around. When you really care, what comes back is always more than what you gave away in the first place. Caring still pays off for me today, in that nearly 100 percent of my consulting, speaking, and training business is the result of repeat business and referrals.

When the woman from the faculty development office pointed out that caring was the secret to my classroom success, I'm sure she had no idea that she had discovered the ultimate secret to personal and professional success. You have to care and if you do, it will show. This is what PRAM is all about and this is what gets people to stand in line just waiting for the chance to do you a favor.


## PATIENCE


Whenever we apply any new technique or process, whether for selling, managing, or motivating, most of us expect instant results. The continued popularity of fad diets serves as a tribute to this quick fix mentality. This final concept, patience, is probably the most difficult to apply. The PRAM Model is anything but a quick fix. Rather, it's a sure fix and a lasting fix. It doesn't produce instant results, but it does produce phenomenal results.

A customer can only be turned into an enthusiastic salesperson on your behalf *after* you have taken him or her through all four steps of the PRAM Model. Furthermore, you must take each customer through the PRAM Model one step at a time over a period of time. You can't expect all this to happen in one or two quick sales calls any more than you can expect to make a serious marriage commitment after one or two half-hour dates. That's not the way people work. Developing trust takes time and has to occur at a natural and comfortable pace. Remember, Ronald Reagan became the most successful president in history at getting his proposed legislation passed because he did not propose one piece of legislation until *after* he had spent many months taking certain key members of the House and Senate through all four steps of the PRAM Model. After that he made it look easy and left the members of the news media scratching their heads, trying to figure out his magic formula for success.

When it comes to turning your customers into a sales force, patience really is a virtue. Shortly after I returned from Vietnam, I entered the doctoral program in business administration at Michigan State University. As the money I received from the G.I. Bill only covered a fraction of the cost of going to school, I joined an Army Reserve unit in order to make up the difference. I was then given command of the unit, which meant that I was responsible for everything regarding that unit, including recruiting.

The unit I took over was supposed to have 104 people in it. After I performed a personnel audit, I found that it only had 54 people on its rolls. In addition, 26 of these remaining 54 were getting out of the Army Reserve within six months. And the draft had just ended, which was the biggest reason people joined reserve units during the Vietnam era. Just when I thought things couldn't get any worse, the next day a general from Indianapolis came up and informed me that if I didn't bring my unit up to full strength within six months, I would be relieved of my command.

At this point, I really wanted to tell this insensitive general what he could do with his reserve unit, but my reputation was important to me and I didn't want a black mark on my service record. So I decided I would give it a go and try to recruit the necessary 76 people. Talk about a tough sell! Just try to get someone to sign up to be hassled at least one weekend a month and two weeks each summer for six years, when there is no draft, in the relatively small city of Lansing, Michigan, just as the Vietnam war is winding down and anti-military sentiment is high. Even if someone were to take you up on such a deal, you'd have to question their sanity!

However, I decided to take recruiting these 76 people as a personal challenge. I started by ensuring that I was taking very good care of the people who were already in my unit in the hopes that some of them would reenlist or bring their friends. This meant straightening out any pay problems without delay, making sure we had warm tents and hot food when we went to the field, seeing to it that people were promoted on time or even ahead of time if they deserved it, and in general, going to bat for them when they encountered problems. I also took an interest in each individual personally. We spent a lot of time after meetings talking about careers and what the future might hold in store for each of us.

I took a similar approach with potential new recruits. Instead of trying to sign them up immediately, I got to know them first. I also made it a point to go to their homes and get to know members of their families. In a number of cases, these potential recruits would have a friend or two at their homes when I made these visits. We would talk about the future, about the army or anything these people were interested in, but I never tried to sell people on signing up for the Army Reserve while I was on one of these visits. All of this visiting did consume a large amount of time, but I enjoyed getting to know all these people. I wasn't sure if there was going to be a payoff because during the first four-and-a-half months, I recruited only 11 people. But during the next six weeks, 71 people signed up! It was amazing. One person walked into my office with 13 of his friends, all of whom wanted to enlist in my unit. A dozen others brought at least one friend with them when they signed up.

If you only observed what went on during those last six weeks, it looked like I had a natural gift for attracting and selling people. They came in from all directions almost begging for a chance to become part of my unit. What wouldn't have been apparent, however, was that during the preceding four-and-a-half months, I took nearly every one of those people through all four steps of the PRAM Model, one step at a time. Yes, it was a lot of work and took a lot of time, but the payoff was phenomenal.

These same kinds of results can be yours, but only if you apply the PRAM Model to your customers with the patience required to allow the process to occur naturally and comfortably. When you apply the PRAM Model in this manner, you're no longer selling; rather, you're making it easy for your customers to buy. Instead of merely landing the order, you're going to land the business.

# CHAPTER TEN

# Making It Happen

So how do you go about turning your customers into a sales force? You need only to remember four things. First, force yourself to take some time and do some planning. Whenever you come into contact with a current or potential customer, client, or patient, always ask yourself, "What can I do for this person that will motivate him to do what I want done in return?"

Second, recognize that customers buy from people, not companies or agencies. Furthermore, these customers are very willing to give repeat business and refer their friends to people they know and trust. Thus, it's important that you spend the necessary time building relationships with the people who stand between you and success or failure.

Third, make sure the agreements you reach with your customers are truly Win-Win. That is, your customers get what they want by helping you get what you want.

Finally, don't overlook the maintenance aspect of the PRAM Model. When someone goes the extra mile for you, shock them with the way in which you express your gratitude and continually show them that you don't take them for granted.

If you follow these four steps within the context of balance, integrity, and patience, you'll find that your job as a salesperson will be transformed from beating on doors and pounding the pavement to one of managing your customers as your own personal sales force. When this occurs, your productivity as a salesperson will take off like a rocket. You'll achieve high levels of success with less effort and less stress than you've ever imagined, because you've got all your customers standing in line just waiting for a chance to help you become even more successful. And when you see your customers starting to line up just for the privilege of doing you a favor, this should tell you that you've not only found, but you have mastered, the universal secret to successful selling!

# INDEX

## A

Agreement(s)
  customer needs in, 60–63
  finalizing, 69–70
  implementing, 64–65
  maintaining, 21–24, 72–81
  mutual problem solving in,
    65–67
  in Win-Win Negotiation, 17–
    20
Airlines
  American, 21–22
  customer satisfaction with,
    76–78
  People Express, 98–99
  Vingressor, 38
Alessandra, Tony, on customer
  objections, 96
American Airlines, 21–22
American Society for Training
  and Development, 96
Amos, Wally "Famous," selling
  strategy of, 29–30
Appreciation, for customer, 78–
  81
Arizona State University,
  faculty development at,
  107–109
Army Reserve, recruiting
  practices of, 110–111

## B

Bacon, Frank, on customer ego,
  67
Balance, in PRAM Model, 103–
  106
Bill King's Brake-O, 101
Bonding, in relationship
  building, 51–53
*Business Week*, 61
Butler, Tom, on customer ego, 67
Buyer's remorse, prevention of,
  72–75

## C

Carter, Jimmy, personal
  relationships of, 45–46
Cialdini, Bob, on first
  impressions, 51
Cold calls, PRAM Model for, 94–
  95
Commitment, in maintaining
  agreements, 21–24
Customer(s)
  desired responses from, 36–37
  ego of, 67–69
  expressing appreciation for,
    78–81
  identification of, 31–36
  irate, 97–100

# ABOUT THE AUTHOR

ROSS R. RECK, PH.D., is an author, speaker, and consultant, and the president of Ross Reck and Associates, a Phoenix-based management development and consulting firm.

DR. RECK is coauthor of *The Win-Win Negotiator*, published by Pocket Books in 1989. A compelling and dynamic speaker, Dr. Reck has been featured at hundreds of meetings, conferences, and conventions.

Dr. Reck received his Ph.D. in 1977 from Michigan State University. From 1975 to 1985, he served as a professor of management at Arizona State University. Since 1985, Dr. Reck has dedicated himself full-time to spreading his Win-Win message.

Inquiries regarding Ross Reck's availability to speak to your group, meeting, conference, or convention should be addressed to:

Ross Reck and Associates
P. O. Box 26264
Tempe, Arizona 85285-6264
(602) 820-7700